WHAT IS YOUR DESTIN

WHAT IS YOUR DESTINATION?

MARVIN J. ASHTON

Deseret Book Company   Salt Lake City, Utah   1978

Library of Congress Cataloging in Publication Data

Ashton, Marvin J   1915-
    What is your destination?

    Includes index.
    1.   Christian life—Mormon authors.   I.   Title.
BX8656.A83   248′49′3   78-14982
ISBN 0-87747-719-1

To
Norma

John and Patty
Jonne and Dale
Steve and Wendy
Janice and Leif

Acknowledgments

The author is grateful to his secretary, Marilyn Mismash, for her many after-hours contributions in helping prepare this manuscript. He also expresses appreciation to Wm. James Mortimer, Lowell M. Durham, Jr., and Eleanor Knowles of Deseret Book for their help and encouragement in the publication of *What Is Your Destination?*

Contents

Foreword

It is a privilege for me to add a few words of commendation to Elder Marvin J. Ashton as some of his excellent talks are brought together in this helpful book.

Each of us has been helped many times in our lives by those who are willing to listen and give sound counsel. Elder Ashton is one of those rare leaders who both listens and counsels. Thousands of lives, young and old, have been blessed by the wisdom of this noble man, wonderful apostle, and friend.

Elder Ashton has been a servant of the people as long as I have known him. His life literally is devoted to helping others seek out and reach righteous destinations. He teaches by patient encouragement and by quiet example. A Church leader who is not afraid to speak the truth, he counsels as directly and straightforwardly as he knows how. His words are not decorated with fancy trappings—they are charged with wisdom, integrity, practical good sense, and the Spirit of the Lord. He is known as one who gets the job done effectively and without delay. He has handled some of the most sensitive matters for the Church with tact and superb diplomacy. He is comfortable with prisoners or prophets.

How fortunate we are that these great discourses have now been gathered together in this volume so each of us has the opportunity to learn how he can reach his destination—eternal life—with courage and obedience to the gospel. Elder Ashton has walked the path himself; he draws from a wealth of knowledge and experience.

I commend to all the reading of these great messages. They will help all of us to evaluate where we are now, where we ought to be headed, and how we can gain the courage to obey the laws that will help us to arrive.

President Spencer W. Kimball

What Is Your Destination?

A few years ago in England, I was traveling by train from Manchester to Leicester. After about an hour and a half of reading, I put down my books, looked out the window, and wondered if we were getting close to the station. A few minutes later the door to the compartment opened and the conductor entered. "What is your destination?" he asked me. Inasmuch as I had been giving some thought to arrivals, departures, and stops, I answered, "I have an appointment in Leicester." To this he responded, "We shall be at your destination in ten minutes."

After he punched my ticket and left, I pondered his comments, "What is your destination?" and "We shall be at your destination in ten minutes." He seemed convinced that every time the train stopped and dozens or hundreds of people got off, they had arrived at their destinations. Apparently he had been announcing this to his passengers for years. However, I knew, despite his comments, that though I needed to be in Leicester for two days for quarterly conference sessions, Leicester was not my destination. Other cities in England where I would visit were not my destination either. They were all assignments along the way. I had not arrived when I reached any of them.

Having given this thought some consideration over

the years, I am concerned that many of us are confused in our life's travels with destinations, arrivals, stops, calls, stations, and assignments. It appears to me that some of us may be lost today because we think we have arrived.

I would like to share with you some observations and raise some questions within the framework of this question, "What is your destination?"

Have you arrived when you go to the temple? Is temple marriage your destination? Over the years I have heard hundreds of my young associates say, "I want to make the temple. A temple marriage is my goal." To qualify one's self to go to the temple is a lofty ambition, a worthy achievement. We need to remind ourselves of its eternal purposes. However, we have not arrived when we share the blessings of the temple.

Oftentimes there are real dangers in our lives when we allow lofty ideals and goals, such as temple marriage, to become ends instead of means. All of our priorities must be properly placed within the framework of eternity, if we are to avoid the stagnations of arriving. To gain exaltation after celestial marriage, continued devotion and righteousness are required. It is a continuing process, not a state of arrival.

Have you arrived when you receive your call to serve in the mission field? Have you reached your destination when you have completed an honorable mission?

I am reminded of a missionary friend who had difficulty remaining busily engaged the last six months of his mission. He had been assigned to labor in a district as a senior companion after having been an assistant to the mission president. In his own words, "I reached my goal when I held that high position of assistant to the president." He had lost his effectiveness temporarily because he had allowed himself to think he had arrived.

A worthily completed mission is a signal accomplishment along life's journey—it is not a destination. It should be fortification for greater personal service and strength. It should more firmly entrench the feet of the missionary in paths that continue onward and upward to eternal happiness. It should prepare him for the enjoyment of pure religion.

What an important day it is in the life of a missionary when he realizes that an honorable release is a commencement! To our fellow missionaries, past and present, we humbly pray you will never allow yourselves the dangerous luxury of self-declaring, "I have given my two years to the Church." If a returned missionary will set his sights high for life, he will generally take the proper steps to get there. A mission can be the happiest two years in a missionary's life if he not only serves his God and fellowmen selflessly, but if he is also walking in truth and preparing himself for eternal progress.

The joy is in the walking and in the traveling in truth, not in anticipated arrival.

Have you reached your destination when you receive a testimony of the truthfulness of the gospel of Jesus Christ by revelation from the Holy Ghost? Sad to say, some, having received a testimony, feel and respond as if they had arrived. What a sad day in the life of any individual when he fails to use this knowledge and conviction of a testimony for dedicated and continued service. A testimony grows as it is shared. With the possession of a testimony comes the obligation to bear witness to the world of this, the Lord's work. A testimony is not a destination; it is a possession for performance.

Have you reached your destination when you are baptized, become an elder, a bishop, a stake president, a Relief Society officer, a seventy, or an apostle? In these days of needed performance and service, it is hoped all of us will emphatically respond to this question with a resounding NO!

Satan and his forces were never more strongly arrayed than today. He is cunning. He is successful. One of the most subtle and effective tools he is using among us today is the convincing of some that they have arrived, they have reached their destination, they have earned a rest, they aren't needed anymore, they are out of danger, they are beyond temptation, and they can take pride in their accomplishments.

"And thus he flattereth them, and leadeth them along until he draggeth their souls down to hell; and thus he causeth them to catch themselves in their own snare. And thus he goeth up and down, to and fro in the earth, seeking to destroy the souls of men." (D&C 10:26-27.)

Let me tell you about a friend of mine who is traveling the true road with purpose and courage. I was visiting in the mission field when Elder Dennis Dean arrived in the Arizona Mission. His appearance in one of our first meetings created an electrifying influence on all present when he guided himself in his wheelchair down the aisle of the chapel. His associates soon learned why he had been found worthy and able to serve a full-time mission. I recall his testimony that day when he let us all know that this was part of his life's hopes and ambitions. He said, "I will do my best to make myself worthy of your trust and confidence. Don't feel sorry for me. Just help me to do what I know I can do with the Lord's help." Later in the day, his newly assigned companion approached me and asked, "What do you do to be a good companion to a wheelchair-restricted elder?" My response after having spent part of the day with Elder Dean was, "You will do well to keep up with him. The real test in the weeks ahead is for you, not him."

Elder Dean, with the love and companionship of an excellent mission president and fellow missionaries, served as a district leader during his two years, bringing the gospel message to hundreds and leading many to the waters of baptism.

As we continue our thinking along the lines of plans,

destinations, goals, arrivals, and commitments, we can learn from two more of my friends. Some of my friends are unusual. They come from unusual places. One evening as I was clearing my desk prior to leaving for home, the telephone rang. A man's voice said, "Brother Ashton, I have permission from the prison authorities to come and visit with you. Will you wait until I get there?"

Frank came and we talked. I asked him, "Now that you are going to be released from the prison in a week, what are your plans? What are you going to do? What are your goals?" He answered, "I have an apartment. I have a full-time job. I have a wonderful sweetheart. I am going to continue my education. I have a church assignment. I have a lot of things I need to do. I am thirty-two years old and I am only a teacher in the priesthood. I want to be an elder before too long." He ended his visit with a request, "Brother Ashton, if I keep myself squared away, will you go to the temple with me in a few months and perform my marriage?"

Contrast this, if you will, with a conversation with another member of the same institution. "What are you going to do when you get out of this place?" I asked. "All I want is out," he snarled back. "I'm here on a phony rap, and I want out." No plans, no goals, no aims, no preparation. All he wants is out, and I am afraid from his attitude he doesn't care how he accomplishes it.

An honorably completed mission, a celestial marriage, a valued testimony, a position of major responsibility in the Church are not destinations in the lives of true Latter-day Saints. They can be important aids in eternal progression, but they will not save us in the kingdom of God. Only living the life of a faithful Latter-day Saint will make that possible. The Lord has told us, "If thou wilt do good, yea, and hold out faithful to the end, thou shalt be saved in the kingdom of God, which is the greatest of all the gifts of God; for there is no gift greater than the gift of salvation." (D&C 6:13.)

What is your destination? As we pursue our journeys, let us ever bear in mind that in life as in train travel, there are stations, departures, calls, and opportunities for being sidetracked and diverted. Our task is to follow that straight and narrow path which leads to our ultimate destination, eternal life and exaltation in our Father's kingdom.

In the pages of this book I'd like to share with you some of the guideposts and guidelines that will help each of us to achieve that goal. We are eternal, and God never intended for us to travel alone. Wise is the individual who follows in the Savior's paths, and safety and joy belong to those who will come and follow him.

You Can Get There from Here

A bewildered and confused young man in a huge city had lost his way. In desperation he stopped a man on the sidewalk and said, "How do I get to such and such a destination from here?" After considerable thought, with the skyscrapers, dense traffic, confusing streets, winding rivers, freeways, bridges, and tunnels in mind, the man said, "You can't get there from here."

I have often thought of this advice as I have contemplated particularly some of our youth in their present locations in life. Some are lost, bewildered, confused, scared, sick, insecure, and discouraged. What a tragedy to be in these straits and to be told, in answer to the question "How can I get to where I want to go," "You can't get there from here."

The disciples of the devil teach there is no way back. Live it up, everybody is doing it, be with the in-group, and it's more fun to stay lost, they say. The devil is an enemy to the ways of God, and enticeth to sin. "Wherefore, all things which are good cometh of God; and that which is evil cometh of the devil; for the devil is an enemy unto God, and fighteth against him continually, and inviteth and enticeth to sin, and to do that which is evil continually." (Moroni 7:12.)

What a happy day it will be when, in contrast to the experience the lost young man had in the big city, he or others can find someone who will say, "Yes, you can get there from here. Come, follow me."

I humbly, but with all the power in my possession, declare to our "lost" youth, young men and young women, worldwide, you can make it back from where you are. The welfare services programs of the Church are geared toward helping our young people who have social and emotional problems find their way back to joy and stability.

Be not deceived. God loves you. He cares about you. He wants you back in his paths, where there is comfort, companionship, and purpose. We as leaders need to effectively communicate to our youth that God loves them. We need to sacrifice our time and talents in this direction.

May I share briefly a few experiences of some of our friends who are proving you can get there from where you are.

Henry Hanson (not his real name), a friend of mine, has been confined to the Utah State Prison. He told me, "I don't want to blame anyone back home for my being in prison, but it is a fact that I had no family relationships. I have been involved in the family home evening program at the prison. Without the people who have been assigned to me through this program, many times I would have given up. These people have loved me as if I were their own son. I have never had that, even when I was a small boy. Now, with their help and others, I believe I can make it back a day at a time. I am not proud of being in prison, but I am proud of my experiences while being there. We have a tendency to blame others. We don't want to blame our parents for not loving us, because we know they do, but maybe they didn't have the guidance and direction in their lives to apply when they were bringing us up."

Perhaps in the minds of many of us, Henry would be justified in believing he couldn't make it back. He had detoured too long. But he doesn't believe that. Instead, he is thankful to those who are presently helping him, and is sincerely grateful for the direction in which his life is moving today. He is determined to make it back from where he is.

During a visit to a juvenile detention home some time ago, my attention was drawn to three young girls who were visiting with each other just prior to a religious service. They appeared to be ten to twelve years of age. I found later they were being detained for a few days to see if some problems could be resolved. As I was waiting to participate with them and others in the services, they seemed to be involved in serious conversation. "What could they be talking about?" I wondered to myself. My curiosity prompted me to step closer to them for a chance to catch a few of their words. I was moved when I heard one of the girls say, "I wonder if someone will come today who will want to take me home. It would be fun to live with someone who wants me." Here was a ten-year-old who wasn't wanted. Her parents had given the impression to those in charge that they were pleased when she was confined, because they were then free from putting up with her. What a pleasure it was later to learn she had been placed in a new home by licensed social services agents of the Church, had been adopted, and was loved and receiving parental direction. Loving foster parents are now helping her find her way in the warmth of family unity and oneness.

Many drug abusers are desperately trying to find their ways back today. The road is difficult, the challenge tremendous, but many are making it, thanks to friends and volunteer members who are concerned, caring, and understanding. Often our glances, hasty comments, and lack of patience convey the message, "You are hopeless. You can't get back from here." After I visited for more than three hours with one of our young women who has been lost to drugs for many months, the

9

only encouraging remark she made was, "Thanks for not chewing me out." Two visits later she asked, "Do you think I would make a good schoolteacher?" To a sincere yes, she said, "Thanks, I'll try. I'm only three semesters away from getting my teaching certificate." This girl is making it back. Someone believes in her. Someone has convinced her that she can get there from here. The trip she is on this time will bring her back.

May I challenge all of us, young and old, to vigorously locate and lead those who have temporarily strayed. Let us lead them by our example, love, and persuasion. They deserve our help. They want our direction. They need our love.

How many of us are actively helping the Lord gather his flock? When our Savior declared, "If ye love me, feed my sheep," he wasn't referring to just those found safely in the fold. He needs our help in finding the lost and bringing them back.

The field is white, ready for harvest. The lost want to know how to get back. They want to be shown they can get there from where they are. Let us not give up. Let us not tire. "And let us not be weary in well doing: for in due season we shall reap, if we faint not." (Galatians 6:9.)

The Time Is Now

In response to a recent greeting of, "How are things going?" a long-time acquaintance responded with, "If I can just get through this month, I think things will be all right." This comment reminded me that over the years this has been a continuing attitude with him. I have never heard him express any pleasure or satisfaction in now or today.

This brief association brought to mind a notion commonly shared by many that the best of life is just ahead, over the next hill, a few years away, retirement, tomorrow, next month, when I turn sixteen, or next summer. We become actively engaged in the pastime of conditioning ourselves to believe that happiness and achievement are always somewhere in the future. There is an attitude of tolerating today, even looking past today in anticipation of a better tomorrow. To people so inclined, the better future may never come. The pleasant future belongs to those who properly use today. We need to find the abundant life as we go along. How can we be happy tomorrow if our "nows" are filled with self-inflicted unhappiness and unwise delays?

Generally speaking, those inclined to count their daily blessings have more to count because they help make more possible as they learn gratitude. A constant waiting for a brighter future may cause us to lose the beautiful today. Some spend so much time getting ready to live for an unknown future that they discover there is suddenly no time left to live. Often in our anxiousness for the joys of the future we run away from the very things we are wanting and needing today. An appropriate examination of the passing moment will prove it leads to eternity. We need to constantly remind ourselves that eternity is in process now.

When the wise counsel that "men should be anxiously engaged in a good cause, and do many things of their own free will, and bring to pass much righteousness" (D&C 58:27) was given, the time structure referred only to now, today, and without delay. How unwise are those who want to delay repentance until tomorrow. With each passing day the process becomes more difficult to pursue. Most of our hurts and misunderstandings could be cleared away if treated today instead of waiting for them to go away tomorrow.

To live more fully each hour and to glean the most from each day is wisdom. How unwise we are to waste our todays when they determine the significance of our tomorrows. We should wisely live a day at a time because that is all we have. While our families are available to us we should take time to develop oneness, unity, and character. Girls of today are the women of tomorrow. Boys of today are the men of tomorrow. The kind of men and women we produce for the future depends upon how they are taught to use today. How fortunate a child is to be raised in a home where love, respect, honor, integrity, and commitment are appropriately displayed each day.

If we have good health we should enjoy it. If we do not have good health, we should begin now anxiously trying to improve it. What a thrill it is to see people achieving, conquering, overcoming through proper daily action, self-discipline, and commitment. Progression and achievement belong to those who have learned to use the opportunity of now. Our strides of today will determine our locations tomorrow. Let me share with you an example of the results of daily determination and performance.

In 1960 the Olympics were held in Melbourne, Australia. In the spotlight on the winner's platform one day there stood a beautiful, tall, blonde American girl. She was being presented a gold medal, symbolic of first place in worldwide competition. Tears ran down her cheeks as she accepted the recognition. Many thought she was touched by the victory ceremony; the thing they did not know was the story of her determination, self-discipline, and daily action. At the age of five she had polio. When the disease left her body, she couldn't use her arms or legs. Her parents took her daily to a swimming pool where they hoped the water would help hold her arms up as she tried to use them again. When she could lift her arms out of the water with her own power, she cried for joy. Then her goal was to swim the width of the pool, then the length, then several lengths. She kept on trying, swimming, enduring day after day after day, until she won the goal medal for the butterfly stroke—one of the most difficult of all strokes in swimming—at the Olympics in Melbourne.

What if Shelly Mann had not been encouraged at age five to achieve, continue, and overcome? What a tremendous asset were parents who assisted her in the importance of today and now in preparation for tomorrow.

In recalling some of the Savior's well-known teachings, the word *now* can be appropriately added to emphasize their impact. "If ye love me, keep my commandments"—NOW. (John 14:25.) "Go ye into all the world, and preach the gospel to every creature"—NOW. (Mark 16:15.) "Come, follow me"—NOW. (Luke 18:22.) Truly, if we love God, we will serve him now.

There are those among us, though they would deny

13

it, who are hungry for fellowship and activity in the Church today. They need us and we need them. It is our duty and blessing to help them find the way now. We and they are God's sheep, and we can best be fed and led together. Today is the time to let them know we care and that the Lord loves them. He stands anxious to forgive and welcome in the processes of repentance. God give us the courage to act now.

There is an urgency today for all of us to take time for God. Wise are those who will use God's ways now to insure his eternal companionship tomorrow. The time to become acquainted and know God is today. To achieve true abundance, life must be lived a day at a time in God's companionship.

As we take time for God, we will become more like him. Robert Louis Stevenson once said, "Saints are sinners who kept trying." It was our Savior Jesus Christ who said, "If ye continue in my word, then are ye my disciples indeed." (John 8:31.) The message is loud and clear. If we work, serve, and improve now, each hour, each day will lead us onward and upward to a significant tomorrow in his paths. Today is the time for decision. Now is the time for action.

Believe me when I tell you God is well pleased when he sees us using our time wisely. With some he is not well pleased because they fear being anxiously engaged in his paths. Some who are willing to listen to the prophet's voice are disappointing to God when they lack the courage and desire to apply the counsel now, even today. We make a big mistake when we allow ourselves to believe it will be easier to start back tomorrow than today.

One of the easiest ways back is to come back with others. One of the greatest pleasures we can know is to render special human services on purpose today and let them be found out by accident tomorrow. By adopting this way of life our friends will lift us daily as we see their new attitudes, accomplishments, and enjoy their associations.

What a blessing it would be in so many lives if, just for today, we could look to God instead of gold; if the craze for power, possessions, advantages, and worldly status could be replaced with eternal pursuits and treasures.

When we have plans or tendencies that are money oriented, and we look forward to all the things money will buy, it's a good time to stop and ask if in the pursuit we are losing the things money won't buy. In our daily commitments to money and the accumulation of worldly goods and acclaim, we may be passing by the things we are trying to find. Some who are missing quality life as they go along may well miss it altogether. Remember, tomorrow is connected with today, and what we do with today determines the tomorrow.

"For behold, this life is the time for men to prepare to meet God; yea, behold the day of this life is the day for men to perform their labors. . . . do not procrastinate the day of your repentance. . . ." (Alma 34:32-33.)

The best of life is not just around the corner, when I go on a mission, after marriage, after the house is paid for, after the recession is over, or after the children are raised. The best of life is now. Today is the time to really start living. Today is the time to start on tomorrow. The future belongs to those who know how to live now. There are no unimportant days in the lives of those who are anxiously engaged.

There is a tendency on the part of many today, worldwide, to postpone appropriate actions and commitments until international unrest settles. To those so inclined, may I suggest His business must and does roll forward. It knows no boundaries. The time and climate for action is now. There is an urgency for us to thrust in our sickles and prepare the earth for his purposes.

Listen again with me to his timeless invitation, to his

master touch: "Now as he walked by the Sea of Galilee, he saw Simon and Andrew his brother casting a net into the sea: for they were fishers. And Jesus said unto them, Come ye after me, and I will make you to become fishers of men. And *straightway* they forsook their nets, and followed him." (Mark 1:16-18. Italics added.)

God help us to forsake our procrastinating ways and straightway follow him. Now is the time to serve the Lord. These truths I know better today than I did yesterday.

It Takes Courage

The apostle Paul wrote to the Romans, "For I am not ashamed of the gospel of Christ: for it is the power of God unto salvation to every one that believeth. . . ." (Romans 1:16.)

The kind of courage that motivated Paul is a strength and power for individual growth and accomplishment. Courage prompts positive action. It takes courage to go into all the world and preach the gospel to every creature; to seek first the kingdom of God; to thrust in one's sickle; to gird up our loins and fresh courage take; to walk uprightly before the Lord. Let's look at four areas of courageous conduct in which we can see how important this virtue is in the life of each one of us.

1. *It takes courage to be a Latter-day Saint.*

The Prophet Joseph Smith exhibited unusual courage when some acquaintances early in his church service suggested when the going was extremely difficult, "Give it up, Joe, or it will cost you your life." Can you today see and hear him stand firm and declare he would rather die than deny that which he knew to be true? He stated:

"So it was with me. I had actually seen a light, and in the midst of that light I saw two Personages, and they did in reality speak to me; and though I was hated and persecuted for saying that I had seen a vision, yet it was true; and while they were persecuting me, reviling me, and speaking all manner of evil against me falsely for so saying, I was led to say in my heart: Why persecute me for telling the truth? I have actually seen a vision; and who am I that I can withstand God, or why does the world think to make me deny what I have actually seen? For I had seen a vision; I knew it, and I knew that God knew it, and I could not deny it, neither dared I do it; at least I knew that by so doing I would offend God, and come under condemnation." (Joseph Smith—History 1:25.) We can all thank God for the Prophet's courageous example and life.

Another example of this kind of courage is given by a fine member in Melbourne, Australia, who recalled the first impact the Church had upon him as a nonmember when he was courting a young Latter-day Saint woman. In a very friendly but firm manner she informed him, "If you marry me, it will be in the temple." He said at the time he didn't know what the temple was. Thanks to the courage of a dedicated young lady he found out, and today he serves as a stake president.

2. *It takes courage to be different.*

We are living in a day and age when it is a pattern of life to follow the crowd. Latter-day Saints should be different. They should live according to righteous principles. We are to be in the world but not of the world. Our goals and performances must be lofty and eternal.

"But ye are a chosen generation, a royal priesthood, an holy nation, a peculiar people; that ye should shew forth the praises of him who hath called you out of darkness into his marvellous light." (1 Peter 2:9.)

Correct principles make it possible for us to appropriately govern ourselves in today's communities. Jesus of Nazareth, our Savior, set the example of courageous conviction when he stood before Pilate with his life hanging in the balance.

". . . and the governor asked him, saying, Art thou the King of the Jews? And Jesus said unto him, Thou sayest. And when he was accused of the chief priests and elders, he answered nothing. Then said Pilate unto him, Hearest thou not how many things they witness against thee? And he answered him to never a word; insomuch that the governor marvelled greatly." (Matthew 27:11-14.)

In today's society, a morally clean individual is different. Chastity is not outdated. Youth of the noble birthright will be virtuous and clean—yes, different. They will avoid alcohol, drugs, tobacco, hot drinks, immodesty, poor grooming, and unwholesome music, magazines, movies, and companions. Wicked conduct will never bring happiness. Righteous conduct will bring rejoicing. The psalmist said, "This is the day which the Lord hath made; we will rejoice and be glad in it." (Psalm 118:24.)

"Finally, brethren, whatsoever things are true, whatsoever things are honest, whatsoever things are just, whatsoever things are pure, whatsoever things are lovely, whatsoever things are of good report; if there be any virtue, and if there be any praise, think on these things." (Philippians 4:8.)

3. *It takes courage to stand firm.*

Ever bear in mind that Satan is subtle. Don't be lured into the wicked ways of the world. Stand firm in the right. The Lord loves men and women of integrity who love the right. Of the Prophet's beloved brother Hyrum he said, "And again, verily I say unto you, blessed is my servant Hyrum Smith; for I, the Lord, love him because of the integrity of his heart, and because he loveth that which is right before me, saith the Lord." (D&C 124:15.)

The Lord admonished Oliver Cowdery to stand firm by the Prophet: "Therefore be diligent; stand by my servant Joseph, faithfully, in whatsoever difficult circumstances he may be for the word's sake. Admonish him in his faults, and also receive admonition of him. Be patient; be sober; be temperate; have patience, faith, hope and charity." (D&C 6:18-19.)

With God's help we can stand firm and do all things. We can joyfully say, as did Ammon in the Book of Mormon, "I do not boast in my own strength, nor in my own wisdom; but behold, my joy is full, yea, my heart is brim with joy, and I will rejoice in my God. Yea, I know that I am nothing; as to my strength I am weak; therefore I will not boast of myself, but I will boast of my God, for in his strength I can do all things; yea, behold, many mighty miracles we have wrought in this land, for which we will praise his name forever." (Alma 26:11-12.)

4. *It takes courage to continue.*

"Then said Jesus to those Jews which believed on him, If ye continue in my word, then are ye my disciples indeed; And ye shall know the truth, and the truth shall make you free. They answered him, We be Abraham's seed, and were never in bondage to any man: how sayest thou, Ye shall be made free? Jesus answered them, Verily, verily, I say unto you, Whosoever committeth sin is the servant of sin." (John 8:31-34.)

Those of us who have found the gospel of Jesus Christ in its fulness and purity have the obligation not only to share it with the world, but also to continue faithful in our lives. Having received the blessings, privileges, and strengths of the gospel is not enough. We must valiantly continue, and by so doing be a beacon unto the world as to the fruits of Christ's teachings.

"He that hath my commandments, and keepeth them, he it is that loveth me: and he that loveth me shall be loved of my Father, and I will love him, and will manifest myself to him.

"Judas saith unto him, not Iscariot, Lord, how is it that thou wilt manifest thyself unto us, and not unto the world?

"Jesus answered and said unto him, If a man love me, he will keep my words: and my Father will love him, and we will come unto him, and make our abode with him.

"He that loveth me not keepeth not my sayings; and the word which ye hear is not mine, but the Father's which sent me.

"These things have I spoken unto you, being yet present with you.

"But the Comforter, which is the Holy Ghost, whom the Father will send in my name, he shall teach you all things, and bring all things to your remembrance, whatsoever I have said unto you.

"Peace I leave with you, my peace I give unto you: not as the world giveth, give I unto you. Let not your heart be troubled, neither let it be afraid.

"Ye have heard how I said unto you, I go away, and come again unto you. If ye loved me, ye would rejoice, because I said, I go unto the Father: for my Father is greater than I." (John 14:21-28.)

The Lord has made a special promise to those who continue faithfully: "It shall come to pass that every soul who forsaketh his sins and cometh unto me, and calleth on my name, and obeyeth my voice, and keepeth my commandments, shall see my face and know that I am." (D&C 93:1.) "Greater love hath no man than this, that a man lay down his life for his friends. Ye are my friends, if ye do whatsoever I command you." (John 15:13-14.)

May our Heavenly Father bless us with courage to do the right. Especially may he give us the desire and power to have the courage to be worthy Latter-day Saints, the courage to be different, the courage to stand firm, and the courage to continue.

Love of the Right

There seems to be a tendency among many in our society today to live by compromise, rationalization, comparison, and self-justification. Love of right has been replaced by love of acceptance and convenience. Some mistakenly think the pathway of safety is somewhere between the path of righteousness and the road to destruction. Others seem to have convinced themselves that the way to perfection is reached by traveling the highway of compromise.

One mother referred to the conduct of her college-age son with a mild tone of satisfaction when she said, "He may not do any studying, but at least he isn't participating in campus riots." An inmate of a prison being confined because of a burglary sentence seemed to have a ring of status in his voice when he pointed to another prisoner and said, "At least I'm not as bad as that guy. He's in here for second-degree murder." A shoplifter seemed to feel she was only mildly dishonest because she was caught taking a hat while others have been convicted of stealing dresses. What kind of thinking is exhibited when someone is heard to say, "I may burn up a couple of packages of cigarettes a day, but I'm not on drugs"?

The pressures of the world to conform and experiment are real and mounting upon the young and old alike. Many of us are startled when we learn that there are drug users even among the twelve- and thirteen-year-olds. What should be more shocking are the tactics being used to talk our youth into trying drugs. I have learned from some youths who are entangled in this vicious pastime that such approaches as the following are being widely used: "Drugs are a fun escape from the lousy world in which we live." "Drugs are a friend to the lonely." "Drugs will give you that mature and self-sufficient image so much desired." "Drugs are a people substitute."

I declare with all the forcefulness I possess that these damaging approaches are of the evil one. Young people are being led to believe the "trips" drugs take them on are the safe, "in" way to travel between pious righteousness and destruction.

Drugs are causing many of our young people to drop out before they start. Drugs rob an individual of his sense of values. Drug-tampering youths are playing copy-cat in a subculture element.

May I recommend, as we look at drug abuse or other social problems, that we focus on the causes rather than the symptoms.

When a youth asks himself or a friend, "Why shouldn't I take drugs?" he is very possibly asking the wrong question. What he may really want to know and need to know is, "Why should I want to take *any* kind of stimulant or depressant at all?" "What is there in my life that I am unhappy enough about to want to escape into a diabolic world of illusion?" If we as parents and friends advise our youth that drugs are bad, evil, and immoral, and yet we do not try to understand why they turn to this evil substitute for reality, then the drugs themselves become the issue and not the symptom of the greater issue of unhappiness. We need to know why our loved ones want to run from their present life to the unknown, dangerous life of addiction. What causes a strong, lovely, vibrant young person to allow a chemical to control his or her behavior? What is there at home, school, work, or church that is so uncomfortable that an escape seems necessary?

If we were not faced with the evils of marijuana, LSD, speed, and heroin, we would be faced with some other type of escape mechanism, because some of us as brothers, sisters, parents, friends, and teachers have not yet been able to reach our youth in such a way as to give them the confidence and love they seek. Some of us are not providing the stability in the home, the respect, and the care that every person needs. They need more than church upbringing; they need a loving home life.

Where better can we teach our young people a love for the right than in a happy home situation? Our young people will not want a people substitute if we provide a home atmosphere with loving personal relationships where parents and sisters and brothers really care.

Parents, let's make certain our youth are not continually exposed to the idea that the stresses of daily life require chemical relief. Factual information about drugs should be constantly stressed rather than attempts to frighten or shame. We must try to rear our children so that they are neither deprived of affection nor spoiled. We must give them responsibilities according to their capabilities, and never overprotect them from the difficulties they will encounter. As sure as some adults continue to sow the wind, they will reap the tornado. Let us more firmly entrench ourselves in the true purposes of family life, and sow oneness and reap joy.

When temptations and challenges come there will be painful, trying times not only for youth, but also for parents. Yet then, more than ever, it is imperative that there be love, understanding, and acceptance in the home so our young people can learn that only steadfast pursuit of God's ways will bring a rich, happy life.

It is time for us to reaffirm the great truth that God's

paths are straight. They not only provide safety, but also lead to happiness and eternal progression.

The drug problem is severe today, and the Church is deeply concerned. Families, parents, and Church leaders should do everything possible to prevent or treat these evils. The rise of drug use is almost a subsociety within the larger worldwide society. People, young and old, who are part of the "drug scene" tend to adopt unusual dress, hairstyles, and other mannerisms that set them apart. But unless they become offensive or unacceptable by reason of extreme behavior, we only do harm by rejecting them from our meetings and general fellowship. It is hoped that we will avoid the pitfall of giving excessive publicity to wrong-doers at the expense of the majority who live virtuous lives.

At the same time, we must not react with panic to what is a symptom of greater illness. In fact, there are indications that we have saturated the youth in and out of the Church with information on drugs. We have unintentionally taught them how and where to obtain drugs by our massive campaigns.

The Church recognizes and supports the efforts of reputable people and organizations who are attempting to combat and treat drug problems. Bishops and other priesthood leaders should help drug users find resources of cure and rehabilitation.

When people are curious and tampering with drugs, we should help to strengthen their homes and personal lives through warm, loving reeducation around basic gospel principles. Our youth are looking for purposeful leadership. We need to lead the lost back from where they are. We must teach the others to continue to choose the right and stay on His paths.

Lofty standards of behavior will always be based upon a love for the right. Wickedness in any form will never lead to happiness. We must be aware of those who would have us believe there is no heaven, there is no hell, and the only road to happiness is marked with compromise and convenience. Satan is real and he is effective. Drug abuse is one of his tools. He would throw men down and, by his cunning, have all mankind strangers to God. Let us not be deceived. God lives, and through him and with him we can accomplish all things. We must not permit ourselves to become entangled in the sin of drugs or the sin of compromising our standards; rather, we must learn to avoid all the ways of Satan.

Our Heavenly Father is so concerned that we do right that he will bless each of us with a sign, if we will ask his counsel. Do we realize that he has promised us a physical manifestation if we but ask him to direct us in the right? In the Doctrine and Covenants we have this commitment from the Lord: "But, behold, I say unto you, that you must study it out in your mind; then you must ask me if it be right, and if it is right I will cause that your bosom shall burn within you; therefore, you shall feel that it is right." (D&C 9:8.) We compromise our blessings, we rationalize ourselves out of the sure, safe way, when we do not ask God to guide us in the decisions that are part of our daily lives.

The Lord has promised he will help us in our pursuit of happiness if we will trust in him and follow his path. The abundant life will be ours if we rely on his strength. If we will magnify the priesthood we hold and share our talents every day, Satan will have no power over us and our Heavenly Father's strength will make all righteous things possible. Ammon, in his comments to his brother Aaron, in the Book of Mormon, points to a way of life that brings security: "Yea, I know that I am nothing; as to my strength, I am weak; therefore, I will not boast of myself, but I will boast of my God, for in his strength, I can do all things; . . . for which we will praise his name forever." (Alma 26:12.) All we need to do to enjoy eternal happy lives is to live the gospel of Jesus Christ.

President David O. McKay once stated that "no

other success in life can compensate for failure in the home." I believe we start to fail in the home when we give up on each other. We have not failed until we have quit trying. As long as we are working diligently with love, patience, and long-suffering, despite the odds or the apparent lack of progress, we are not classified as failures in the home. We only start to fail when we give up on a son, daughter, mother, or father.

To our young friends and bewildered parents caught in the vicious grips of drug abuse and its heartaches, I declare to you there is a way back. You can make it. There is hope. I bear witness that a love for that which is right will bring us our Heavenly Father's strength and protection. In his paths we will find security. My prayer is that we will have the desire in our hearts to earnestly seek the pathway of safety from evils such as drugs by honestly keeping all of his commandments.

As we unitedly work to help our youth in combatting and avoiding all of the temptations of the day, may we be reminded, ". . . let every man be swift to hear, slow to speak, slow to wrath: for the wrath of men worketh not the righteousness of God." (James 1:19-20.)

Obey Promptly

One of the greatest blessings man has is the opportunity to be obedient. All of our blessings flow from obedience, which is a cardinal law of heaven. Righteousness and individual growth rest upon it. It is an eternal principle available for the benefit and progress of mankind.

In the Doctrine and Covenants this principle of truth is stated: "Whatever principle of intelligence we attain unto in this life, it will rise with us in the resurrection. And if a person gains more knowledge and intelligence in this life through his diligence and obedience than another, he will have so much the advantage in the world to come. There is a law, irrevocably decreed in heaven before the foundations of this world, upon which all blessings are predicated—and when we obtain any blessing from God, it is by obedience to that law upon which it is predicated." (D&C 130:18-21.)

Father Adam gave us a classical illustration of perfect obedience when the Lord commanded him to offer the firstlings of his flocks as a sacrifice, which he gladly did. Later an angel appeared to him and asked, "Why dost thou offer sacrifices unto the Lord? And Adam said unto him: I know not save the Lord commanded me." (Moses 5:6.)

Our true love of God is measured in terms of

obedience and service, for the Savior has said, "If you love me, keep my commandments." (John 14:15.)

Jesus Christ set a perfect example of obedience for all of us. "Though he were a Son, yet learned he obedience by the things which he suffered; And being made perfect, he became the author of eternal salvation unto all them that obey him." (Hebrews 5:8-9.)

A worthy prayer for all of us today could be, "Help me, O Lord, to obey promptly." Obedience increases personal stature. Obedience increases personal capacity. Obedience helps mankind to know and become like God.

Another worthy personal commitment is this: "Help me, O Lord, to obey thee through thine appointed leaders." *Any* Latter-day Saint not obedient to the leaders of the Church will not have the opportunity to be obedient to the promptings of the Lord. In the Doctrine and Covenants we read: "For all who will have a blessing at my hands shall abide the law which was appointed for that blessing, and the conditions thereof, as were instituted from before the foundations of the world." (D&C 132:5.) To obey the gospel law is to yield obedience to those divinely called to preside over us.

We are living in unsettled and trying times. Much of the unrest and confusion in the world today is caused by man's fear to obey God because of the pressure of man. Certainly if we want peace, progress, and prosperity, it will come through adherence to God's principles. We have no need to fear if we keep God's commandments, for the apostle Peter has taught us, "We ought to obey God rather than men." (Acts 5:29.) Let us commit ourselves to follow our prophet and president and to obey his admonitions. He is most appropriately sustained by our obedience and his leadership according to God's laws.

The Need for Moral Courage

Some time ago I had a stimulating experience as I visited with some young friends. Time was not only taken for group discussions and opinions, but for private talks as well. I learned again that our choice youth want answers. They want direction. They want acceptance. One young lady impressed me with her very sincere plea, "Why can't I be the same every day? Some days I feel like I'm on top of the world; other times I'm discouraged and am low, especially on myself."

We are living in a day when there has never been a greater need for moral courage: courage to continue in righteousness, courage to communicate, courage to have patience, and courage to have childlike faith.

If we are to have *courage to continue in righteousness,* we must also have courage not to be diverted, not to be mis-led, and not to stray, as well as courage to be anxiously engaged in good work. In the Gospel of John we are reminded of the promised blessings in store for those who have the courage to continue: "If you continue in my word, then are ye my disciples indeed; And ye shall know the truth, and the truth shall make you free." (John 8:31-32.)

What a joy it is to be associated with members of the Church, young and old, who are continuing in the paths of righteousness! It is a thrill to see our youth in far-off stakes and missions, as well as those nearby, preparing valiantly for temple marriages. Other thousands inspire us as we see them valiantly continuing in their missionary and military services. God will help us continue in his ways if we humbly seek his guidance. Directing our energies in his pathways will bring blessings of genuine joy and happiness. His way is the right way; the right way is the happy way.

We need the *courage to communicate* through word and deed the great truth, "I am not ashamed of the gospel of Christ: for it is the power of God unto salvation to every one that believeth." (Romans 1:16.) Joseph Smith's prayer in the grove was answered because he had the courage to communicate with unwavering faith. Channels of communication between parents and youth are effectively opened and used as the family circle is strengthened. Where necessary we challenge our youth to take the lead to see that family home evenings are scheduled and held so that they might learn to communicate more purposefully not only with family members, but with their Heavenly Father as well. Many young people have done this in the past, and today their parents love them for it. Family home evenings, properly held, will not only open the channels of communication for family members, but for God's spirit as well. What a pleasure it was recently to hear a beautiful seventeen-year-old girl say, "Dad and I no longer have a communication hang-up. Thanks to family home evenings we are back on the same wave length and are now pretty well tuned in."

One of the greatest blessings that can come to a child of any age is the benefit of being raised in a home where the mother and father love each other. The love of husband and wife should be warm and sincere to provide a priceless environment for their children. Children learn love as they experience it.

Earnest communication with others develops a feeling of belonging. It lets others know we care. Love and compassion are not obsolete or old-fashioned. They are virtues that build understanding and happiness. It is difficult for young people to keep the commandments of God without sharing a feeling of close relationship with their parents and leaders in the Church. Let us look for the best in our children and associates. It is the Lord's will that we build up, not tear down. Our responsibility is to communicate the positive, emphasize the positive, and not be parties to promoting the negative.

We need the *courage to have patience,* understanding, and compassion. From some of our troubled youth in today's complex society, may I humbly pass on these suggestions to parents and leaders: "Don't give up on us. Don't condemn us. Don't resent us. Don't try to get us to conform through sympathy, embarrassment, or ridicule. Instead, give us reasons. Give us examples. Give us your best you." May we as parents and leaders so live and lead as to merit the gratitude of a grateful teenager's "Thank you for helping me to find my way back," or "Thank you for helping me to remain steady." We must learn to lead others through patience, understanding, and love, and to say the encouraging word at the right time and the right place. Good leaders don't give up. Good parents don't give up. Good youth don't give up.

We need the *courage to have childlike faith.* "Therefore, whoso repenteth and cometh unto me as a little child, him will I receive, for of such is the kingdom of God." (3 Nephi 9:22.) We need childlike love, childlike repentance, childlike prayers, and childlike faith. What a warm experience it was to kneel with a Latter-day Saint family in far-away Uruguay, as we shared the thought of an eleven-year-old girl who led us in family prayer. Her spirit touched us as she communed with her Heavenly Father in her native Spanish language. At the conclusion of her lovely prayer, we said to her father, "What was it she said in her prayer about the temple?" He responded,

33

"She said, 'Help me, Heavenly Father, to be good enough in the way I live so that some day I can marry in the temple.' " With this childike faith and daily, sincere preparation, her heart's desire will be possible.

"Verily, thus saith the Lord: It shall come to pass that every soul who forsaketh his sins and cometh unto me, and calleth on my name, and obeyeth my voice, and keepeth my commandments, shall see my face and know that I am." (D&C 93:1.) What a crowning promise to the faithful! What a blessing for those who will continue! What could be a more effective humble prayer for us in this troubled day than to ask our Father in heaven to bless us with courage—the courage to so live that we won't be the same every day, but, with the Lord's help, a little better each day, step by step.

The Power of Prayer

One of the greatest daily evidences we have of God's great love for each of us is in our relationship to him in our prayers. He has invited us to pray constantly. He wants to hear from us. He wants to help us. He wants to guide us. He wants us to be dependent upon him. He wants us to pray always for guidance, strength, and constant protection.

"And now, my beloved brethren, I perceive that ye ponder still in your hearts; and it grieveth me that I must speak concerning this thing. For if ye would hearken unto the spirit which teacheth a man to pray ye would know that ye must pray; for the evil spirit teacheth not a man to pray, but teacheth him that he must not pray.

"But behold, I say unto you that ye must pray always, and not faint; that ye must not perform any thing unto the Lord save in the first place ye shall pray unto the Father in the name of Christ, that he will consecrate thy performance unto thee, that thy performance may be for the welfare of thy soul." (2 Nephi 32:8-9.)

We should never underestimate the power of prayer. The Church of Jesus Christ is on the earth today because God heard the prayers of a fourteen-year-old boy, who humbly knelt in a grove after reading in the Bible: "If any of you lack wisdom, let him ask of God, that giveth to all men liberally, and upbraideth not; and it shall be given him." (James 1:5.)

Joseph Smith later wrote of his experience:

"Never did any passage of scripture come with more power to the heart of man than this did at this time to mine. It seemed to enter with great force into every feeling of my heart. I reflected on it again and again, knowing that if any person needed wisdom from God, I did; for how to act I did not know, and unless I could get more wisdom than I then had, I would never know; for the teachers of religion of the different sects understood the same passages of scripture so differently as to destroy all confidence in settling the question by an appeal to the Bible.

"At length I came to the conclusion that I must either remain in darkness and confusion, or else I must do as James directs, that is, ask of God. I at length came to the determination to 'ask of God,' concluding that if he gave wisdom to them that lacked wisdom, and would give liberally, and not upbraid, I might venture.

"So, in accordance with this, my determination to ask of God, I retired to the woods to make the attempt. It was on the morning of a beautiful, clear day, early in the spring of eighteen hundred and twenty. It was the first time in my life that I had made such an attempt, for amidst all my anxieties I had never as yet made the attempt to pray vocally.

"After I had retired to the place where I had previously designed to go, having looked around me, and finding myself alone, I kneeled down and began to offer up the desire of my heart to God. I had scarcely done so, when immediately I was seized upon by some power which entirely overcame me, and had such an astonishing influence over me as to bind my tongue so that I could not speak. Thick darkness gathered around me, and it seemed to me for a time as if I were doomed to sudden destruction.

"But, exerting all my powers to call upon God to deliver me out of the power of this enemy which had seized upon me, and at the very moment when I was ready to sink into despair and abandon myself to destruction—not to an imaginary ruin, but to the power of some actual being from the unseen world, who had such marvelous power as I had never before felt in any being—just at this moment of great alarm, I saw a pillar of light exactly over my head, above the brightness of the sun, which descended gradually until it fell upon me.

"It no sooner appeared than I found myself delivered from the enemy which held me bound. When the light rested upon me I saw two Personages, whose brightness and glory defy all description, standing above me in the air. One of them spake unto me, calling me by name and said, pointing to the other—*This is My Beloved Son. Hear Him!*" (Joseph Smith—History 1:11-17.)

God answers prayers today in the home, in the office, in the school, on the highway, in the air, in our dating, in our courtships, in our churches and temples, and in our solitude and ponderings.

We must pray constantly that we might know God, his plans, and his love. Daily dependence upon God through prayer brings strength, growth, and personal stature.

In counseling with couples about to marry or those already married, I always suggest daily prayers. There is a peculiar strength and power that comes to a couple united in prayerful communication to God. He will help those who sincerely and worthily invite him into their family circle and personal lives. On a one-to-one basis or as a couple, he will be as close to us as we will allow him to be. All couples as well as families and individuals need to remind themselves that putting themselves into a proper attitude to appropriately pray often supplies the necessary oil for the troubled waters of the day. Personal prayer is not only power, it is preparation.

If we prepare ourselves to do the will of our Father and communicate with him in prayer, he will hear us and give us entrance into his kingdom according to our personal performances. The personal prayers of the righteous and the sincerely repentant are a joy to our Father.

Brigham Young once said, "Prayer keeps a man from sin, and sin keeps a man from prayer." Let us so live that our contrite spirits and humble hearts will make it possible to constantly communicate with God, and may he help us to make our prayers childlike and continuing as we endeavor to walk uprightly in his strength.

Coping with the Unexpected

It is natural to be concerned about those things that come into our lives over which we have no control. When tragedy, sorrow, setback, disappointment, humiliation, wealth, unusual success, acclaim, and recognition come into our lives, what shall we do then? How do we cope with the unexpected? How do we do our best to meet those challenges and situations? Often we say, "I wonder what I would do should that come into my life as it has into the life of a friend." How do we develop attitudes of strength that will see us through life's unexpected challenges?

At the time of John the Baptist and our Savior Jesus Christ, there were also persons who had grave concern over the personal uncertainties of their lives and their futures.

"And the people asked him [John], saying, What shall we do then? . . . Then came also publicans to be baptized, and said unto him, Master, what shall we do? . . . And the soldiers likewise demanded of him, saying, And what shall we do?" (Luke 3:10, 12, 14.)

It is my firm conviction that when joy, sorrow, success, temporary failure, victory, hurt, misunderstanding, and loss come into our lives, what we do with them is the key to the future. What we do with what happens to us is more important than place or situation. We may have

39

stumbled or been grievously hurt, but we have not fallen if we are willing to get back up.

In keeping with the question, "What shall we do then?" may I share some examples of worthy people who have known what to do with God's help when the unexpected has struck. I will introduce them with questions submitted to me by a group of college students.

1. "Sometimes happenings in life are cruel. You prepare, doing everything in your power to ready yourselves for tests and important events, and then the uncontrollable strikes, stripping you of your potential. What shall we do then?"

In responding to this question, may I use one more question given to me: "After much preparation and prayer for our first football bowl game, why does the Lord allow our first-string quarterback to receive injuries early in the contest and reduce our chances of victory as millions of viewers look on? It could have been such a great missionary tool."

Perhaps the best way to answer that question is to review the facts in the game referred to. It is the first quarter, with our team leading 6 to 0. The quarterback injures his shoulder. What shall we do then? Do we quit? No, we rally around a less experienced quarterback. We dig in. We play harder. We give it our all. We press for victory.

The determined men representing the school knew what to do, and thank the Lord they did it. It was a good missionary tool. I saw maturity, I saw character, I saw quality on that football field. I commend the coach and his associates for knowing what to do—and for hanging in there tough.

2. "Recently we have been shocked at the tragic deaths of full-time missionaries. What shall we do as family members and friends, in relationship to our Heavenly Father, when this is allowed to strike us?"

To answer this question, let me tell you about Tony

Sanchez, who served in the Louisiana Shreveport Mission. I never knew Tony Sanchez as a missionary; I only knew him as a patient at the St. Francis Hospital in Honolulu, where he had been taken for treatment following a serious injury he had received while serving in the mission field. He had fallen and broken his back; now he was paralyzed and in the hospital. What could I say to give him comfort and hope? As I walked into his room, I met his mother standing at his side. Tony was completely immobile, unable to talk; the only thing he was able to move at that time was his eyeballs. While I was wondering what I should say to him and his mother, his mother spoke first and said, "Elder Ashton, I have always wanted to be a nurse and I have never had the opportunity. Now I am a nurse to my injured son." Later she said, "Elder Ashton, I hope we will be blessed with the privilege of sending our other son on a mission. Just because we have had this tragedy is no reason our other son should be deprived, is it?"

Following the death of Tony in that hospital a few days later the mother, the father, and the entire family had their desire fulfilled. Tony's brother James was called to go to South America on a mission. It was interesting that when someone said, "Could I help with funds for James's mission," his family said, "No. We have a little money left over from Tony's insurance and that is going toward his brother's mission." This is a tremendous example of courage and character in action. What shall we do then? The Sanchez family knew well what to do and did it.

3. "I am about to marry. My husband-to-be and I want nothing more than continuing happiness throughout our marriage. We know unforeseen challenges and even disappointments may come. If tragedy strikes our marriage, what shall we do then?"

In December 1974 Sister Zina Card Brown, wife of Elder Hugh B. Brown of the Council of the Twelve, passed away. At the time they had been married sixty-six years. Let me share Elder Brown's thoughts expressed just a few weeks before her passing:

"Eight years ago my sweetheart, Zina, suffered a massive stroke that took her speech and left her paralyzed. The doctors said she probably would not survive the week. As our children surrounded her bed, I pleaded with the Lord to spare her life. Then I spoke to her, though she was unconscious. I reminded her that through the years of our married courtship we had planned and hoped to take the final trip together. I told her I wanted what was best for her and our Father's will, but life would seem empty without her presence.

"I think the Lord in his mercy permitted Zina her choice—she could travel on into immortality and rest, or remain to bless us with her exhibition of quiet faith, patience, and fortitude. Characteristically, she chose to do what she knew would give me the greatest comfort, unmindful of her own tribulation. Hers is truly a Christlike love. Our entire family has been blessed and benefited by her unselfish sacrifice in our behalf. Noble characters do not alone bear trouble; they use it."

4. "Some of our closest friends are not totally committed to the Church. The men don't honor their priesthood and the women are only conveniently active. We like them for what they are. We don't want to strain our choice relationships. Talk seems to do no good at all. What shall we do then?"

Shortly before Christmas one year, I had the opportunity of going to the hospital at the request of a mother whose fifty-five-year-old son was seriously ill. As I met with them and tried to give them comfort, the patient's nephew was in the hospital room as well. The afflicted one's wife said, "Elder Ashton, would it be possible for you to give my husband a blessing?" I said yes. Then I looked in the direction of the thirty-year-old nephew and said, "Are you an elder?" He said, "Yes, I am an elder, but don't ask me to put my hands on his head. I am not worthy to participate in a blessing with you." As he backed away, I said, "Randy, how would you like to try to be worthy for ten minutes? Couldn't you be worthy for that long while you help me give this needed blessing?" He nodded his head and said, "I think I can be worthy for a few minutes." While he was coming over to the side of the bed I said, "If you can do it for ten minutes, you can do it for thirty minutes." He said, "Yes." I said, "If you can do it for thirty minutes, you can do it for a day, can't you?"

About then I felt he figured we had better get on with the blessing or he would be committed. We gave his uncle a blessing and when it was over he said, "Thank you for letting me share this blessing with you. No one has ever put it up to me like this before. I will try to be worthy."

Perhaps the best way to help some of our associates who are not quite as active as they should be is to involve them. I don't know of anything that would be more important and have more impact upon an inactive person than to have us call and say, "Would you help me to administer to my wife, my roommate, or my friend?" We need to give them an opportunity to make shaping up a process.

5. "Terminal illnesses, such as cancer, seem to be striking with more frequency among our age group. We fast, pray, and try to help families so afflicted, but feel so helpless. What shall we do then?"

May I share a mother's comment as she was nursing her twenty-nine-year-old daughter, Christine Jacobsen Cannon, who was gravely ill with cancer. The mother said, "We thank our Heavenly Father we have had her for all of this year. We count each day a bonus. How close we have become during her critical illness. We are filling every hour with the most we can." I had the opportunity of seeing faith, courage, character, and fight in one so sorely afflicted with this terminal disease. I express my thanks for what she did for me in exhibiting the answer to what shall we do then, and my appreciation for a quality mother, Rosebud M. Jacobsen, who taught me well in her hours of coping with the unexpected.

6. "I have been somewhat successful in school with grades, popularity, leadership recognition, and so forth. I am proud and pleased with these developments, but I am concerned about becoming self-sufficient and even arrogant. When I feel the dangers of these possibilities, what shall I do then?"

I am reminded of what President Spencer W. Kimball said at the dedication of the Washington Temple: "Bless all people, our Father, that they may prosper, but not more than their faith can stand. . . . Our Father, in blessing thy people with prosperity, we pray that they may not be surfeited with flocks and herds and acres and barns and wealth which could bring them to worship these false gods." (*Ensign,* February 1975, p. 82.)

Taking freedom with President Kimball's admonition, may I, for our purpose here, say, "Oh God, do not bless us with more stocks, bonds, properties, automobiles, or credit cards than our faith can stand or more than our parents can bear." A worthy prayer might be, "Dear God, in all the days ahead, please bless me with what I need and can stand, not with what I want."

7. "With each passing day I miss my mother more. She was taken from us in death when I was ten. I know it is not wise, but on occasion I allow myself pity and poor performance excuses for this loss in my life. When I get in these moods, what shall I do then?"

A friend of mine lost his mother when he was eleven. He almost died at thirteen with typhoid fever. In his teens smallpox almost took him. Later cancerous throat conditions and an operation took away his voice. Bell's palsy of the face muscles followed this affliction. Heart deterioration made heart surgery necessary at age seventy-seven. Do you know who my friend is? President Spencer W. Kimball. I bear witness that one of the reasons he is a prophet is that with God's help, under every condition, he has known what to do.

As we go through the rest of the days of our lives, now is the time for decision making. What are we going to do about it? When tomorrow comes with challenges, opportunities, successes, joys, or disappointments, we must be ready to perform effectively when "what shall we do then" becomes now.

We are all different. God in his wisdom has so created us. Only *we* can determine what we will do with what happens to us. What we do with what happens to us is more important than what happens to us. Certainly with God's help we can do what is right.

What shall we do then? Let us resolve to so live that the Lord can say to us as he did to the Prophet Joseph Smith in some of his darkest, most trying hours: "My son, peace be unto thy soul; thine adversity and thine afflictions shall be but a small moment; And then, if thou endure it well, God shall exalt thee on high; thou shalt triumph. . . ." (D&C 121:7-8.)

God lives. He is our Father. He knows us. He stands ready to help us. He has placed us here in life to see what we will do under all conditions and situations. It is a time of trial, tribulation, and testing. Often we would prefer to have "this cup pass" rather than go through the consequences. We must never lose sight of the fact that often success, popularity, and fame are more difficult to live with than uneventful calm or even tragedy. "Though he were a Son, yet learned he obedience by the things which he suffered." (Hebrews 5:8.)

We came into this life for experience, and that's all we can take out of it. Thank God we have the right to decide personally and individually what we shall do then. The future does belong to those who know what to do with it. We must look forward to the unknown with optimism and confidence; look to tomorrow with happy expectancy, realizing that with God's help we can do all things.

Act, Don't React

Years ago a wise friend and I were out walking, and we passed one of his neighbors standing in the front yard of his home. My friend greeted the man with, "How are you, Bill? It's good to see you." To this greeting, Bill didn't look up. He didn't even respond.

"He's an old grouch today, isn't he?" I said.

"Oh, he's always that way," my friend responded.

"Then why are you so friendly to him?" I asked.

"Why not?" responded my mature friend. "Why should I let him decide how I am going to act?"

I hope I will never forget the lesson of that evening. The important word was *act*. My friend *acted* toward people. Most of us *react*. At the time it was a strange attitude to me, because I was in grade school and following the practice of, "if you speak to an acquaintance and he does not respond, that is the last time you have to bother," or "if someone shoves you on the school playground, shove him back."

I have thought many times since this experience that many of us are perpetual reactors. We let other people determine our actions and attitudes. We let other people determine whether we will be rude or gracious, depressed or elated, critical or loyal, passive or dedicated.

Do you know people who are cool toward an acquaintance because last time they met he wasn't warm in his greeting? Do you know people who have quit praying to the Lord because he hasn't answered (so they think) their prayers of last month or last year? Do you know people who give up on others because they don't respond in the ways we think they should? Do you know people who fail to realize that Christlike behavior patterns encourage us to be the same yesterday and forever?

The perpetual reactor is an unhappy person. His center of personal conduct is not rooted within himself, where it belongs, but in the world about him. Some of us on occasion seem to be standing on the sidelines waiting for someone to hurt, ignore, or offend us. We are perpetual reactors. What a happy day it will be when we can replace hasty reaction with patience and purposeful action.

I am acquainted with a man who has a brother serving time in a state penitentiary. On several occasions I have asked this friend of mine to accompany me to visit his confined family member. When asked most recently, he responded with an emphatic, "No, I don't want to go. It's no use. He won't talk. He won't listen. He's no good. He will never change." His last statement, "He will never change," prompted me to add mentally, "and apparently neither will you."

This man is allowing his confined brother to control his actions; in fact, he has created a negative attitude in his relationship. The free man has not maintained a positive drive to do what he feels is right; instead, his brother has set the pace for both of them—no communication, no visits, no change in either life.

What a pleasure it is today to be part of a great action program in the Church that makes it possible for us to take people with social problems from the level we find them and help them move forward. Our concern must be to impress our associates with the fact that there is a better tomorrow, and it belongs to those who live for it! Forgiveness and repentance are action principles. What a blessing it is in our lives when we come to realize there is hope and help for all of us in the days ahead, regardless of where we find ourselves at this hour.

When Jim Lovell of *Apollo 13* radioed across almost a quarter of a million miles of space to Houston, Texas, that something had gone wrong in his spacecraft, he taught the world a mighty lesson with his statement: "We've got a problem." Here were three brave men on a voyage to the moon faced with the staggering realization that they might never see the earth again. Something had gone wrong. What should they do now? Act or react? Instead of demanding "Who's responsible for this error," his statement, "We've got a problem," rallied others to their support. When Jim Lovell and his crewmates were later asked if they had fears of not reaching earth again, they responded that they just concentrated on the jobs they had to do. They did everything in their power to get back to earth. They had a terrifying problem, but they were determined to handle it one step at a time, and they hoped and prayed their efforts would succeed. Through action they overcame fear; through action and teamwork they triumphed. What happened is history, but the lesson of action is for our use today.

Shakespeare had a glimpse of the importance of man's personal action when he wrote the following lines in the play *Hamlet:*

> *This above all: to thine ownself be true,*
> *And it must follow, as the night the day,*
> *Thou canst not then be false to any man.*

Being true to ourselves can mean knowing where we are, where we are going, and why, and assisting our associates in traveling the right paths with us.

The Prophet Joseph Smith was a man of action. Torture, belittlement, and all manner of inhumane affliction, including a pending martyr's death, did not halt

49

nor even slow down his life of purposeful action. He acted as one totally committed to the principle, "I am not ashamed of the gospel of Christ, for it is the power of God unto salvation." (Romans 1:16.) He didn't just think about the gospel or react to it; he lived it. He was true to himself and to those principles he valued more than life itself.

The gospel of Jesus Christ is purposeful action. *Ask, seek, knock, judge not,* and *love* are words of action, not reaction. Jesus led his fellowmen as a mighty master because "he taught them as one having authority, and not as the scribes." (Matthew 7:29.) Jesus was true to himself and to his Father and, so important to all of us, he was true to us.

How weak the following reaction philosophies are: "See if your neighbor loves you first before you manifest love toward him." "See if your acquaintance is friendly before you offer your friendship." How powerful is the action commandment, "Thou shalt love thy neighbour as thyself."

We start to fail in our homes when we give up on a family member. We fail in our positions of leadership when we react by saying, "It's no use, they won't come." "It's no use, they won't respond." Let us thrust in our sickles with all of our might in the fields in which we have been called, and not spend our time reacting to the location or type of crop we have been called to harvest.

I humbly pray that we may be men and women of action, and not let anyone else lead us from His paths. If we follow the teachings of the gospel of Jesus Christ to the fullest of our ability, it can truthfully be said of us, through our actions also, that we "increased in wisdom and stature, and in favour with God and man." (Luke 2:52.)

Love Takes Time

A friend of mine recently shared what he considered to be a choice learning experience. It was provided by his young son. Upon returning home from his day's work, this father greeted his boy with a pat on the head and said, "Son, I want you to know I love you."

The son responded with, "Oh, Dad, I don't want you to love me, I want you to play football with me." Here was a boy conveying a much-needed message. The world is filled with too many of us who are inclined to indicate our love with an announcement or declaration.

True love is a process. True love requires personal action. Love must be continuing to be real. Love takes time. Too often expediency, infatuation, stimulation, persuasion, or lust are mistaken for love. How hollow, how empty if our love is no deeper than the arousal of momentary feeling or the expression in words of what is no more lasting than the time it takes to speak them. A group of college students recently indicated to me that their least favorite expression to come from us as the older set is, "If there is ever anything I can do to help you, please let me know." They, as do others, much prefer actions over words.

We must at regular and appropriate intervals speak and reassure others of our love and then take the time necessary to prove it by our actions. Real love does take

51

time. The great Shepherd had the same thoughts in mind when he taught, "If you love me, keep my commandments" (John 14:15) and "Feed my sheep" (John 21:16). Love demands action if it is to be continuing. Love is a process. It is not a declaration, not an announcement, not a passing fancy. It is not an expediency or a convenience. "If ye love me, keep my commandments" and "Feed my sheep" are God-given proclamations that should remind us we can often best show our love through the processes of feeding and keeping.

From a young man confined in a state penitentiary, we can learn more about the process of love. In a most moving letter, he makes an effort to analyze what led to his present situation and all the accompanying agonies. He writes, "My dad never seemed to love me and yet he made big deals of saying 'I love you' and kissing and all, but I learned that 'I love you' meant you didn't have to do anything. I mean, we were never forced to do chores regularly, given no morals or spiritual training at all. To this very day I don't know what principles my parents stand for."

From the father's viewpoint, can't he be credited with feeding and keeping? And hadn't his son been the beneficiary of having a roof over his head, protected from the elements day and night over the years? In responding, I would point out to this mother and father and others that feeding is more than providing food. No man can effectively live by bread alone. Feeding is providing by love adequate nourishment for the entire man—physically, mentally, morally, and spiritually. Keeping is a process of care, consideration, and kindness appropriately blended with discipline, example, and concern. Keeping is more than providing four walls and a roof. All of us need to be constantly reminded that it takes a heap of living and loving to make a house a home.

How do we best show our love? How do we prove our

love? Peter was effectively taught by the Master Teacher how he could best prove his love:

"This is now the third time that Jesus shewed himself to his disciples, after that he was risen from the dead.

"So when they had dined, Jesus saith to Simon Peter, Simon, son of Jonas, lovest thou me more than these? He saith unto him, Yea, Lord; thou knowest that I love thee. He saith unto him, Feed my lambs.

"He saith to him again the second time, Simon, son of Jonas, lovest thou me? He saith unto him, Yea, Lord; thou knowest that I love thee. He saith unto him, Feed my sheep.

"He saith unto him the third time, Simon, son of Jonas, lovest thou me? Peter was grieved because he said unto him the third time, Lovest thou me? And he said unto him, Lord, thou knowest all things; thou knowest that I love thee. Jesus saith unto him, Feed my sheep." (John 21:14-17.)

When were you last fed by a family member or friend? When were you last given nourishment for growth with ideas, plans, sharing of fun, recreation, sorrow, anxiety, concern, and meditation? These ingredients can be shared only by someone who loves and cares. Have you ever gone to extend sympathy and comfort in moments of death and trial, only to come away fed by the faith and trust of the loving bereaved? Certainly the best way for us to show our love in keeping and feeding is to take the time to prove it hour by hour and day by day. Our expressions of love and comfort are empty if our actions don't match. God loves us to continue. Our neighbors and families love us if we will but follow through with sustaining support and self-sharing. True love is as eternal as love itself. Who is to say the joys of eternity are not wrapped up in continuous feeding, keeping, and caring? We need not weary in well-doing when we understand God's purposes for his children.

Undoubtedly our Heavenly Father tires of express-
sions of love in words only. He has made it clear through
his prophets and his word that his ways are ways of commitment, not conversation. He prefers performance over
lip service. We show our true love for him in proportion
to our keeping his words and the processes of feeding.

Let me share with you two examples, not too uncommon, of people who, hour by hour, day by day, and
month by month, have taken the time to love one
another. I say these examples are not too uncommon because, gratefully, all around us we see true love in action.
I'm thinking first of a mother who, through death, suddenly was left without a husband. With her are three
sons ranging in age from early teens to almost missionary
age. Through the years, by example and hard work, she
has independently provided finances, encouragement,
and unity. The feeding and keeping processes have
resulted in the development of three great missionaries,
students, husbands, and fathers. One recently remarked,
"Mother has always taken the time to show her love."
She continues the true processes of love today as her sons
pursue higher education and the opportunities of rearing
their own families.

Some time ago we were attracted to the skills and attitude of a local building contractor. His desire for
perfection and his pride in his work led us to ask questions and get acquainted. As a young man he was left as
the sole supporter of several younger brothers and sisters.
Formal education was of a necessity terminated at the
eighth grade. Shortly after his brothers and sisters were
able to make their own ways, he married. A year after
marriage his wife was afflicted with what was to become
a long pattern of serious illness. For twenty-five years, as
her health steadily worsened, he cared for her and their
two sons. Operations were performed and expenses ran
high, but he worked, cared, and loved without reservation. After the visit we knew we had met a man. Yes,

love takes time. Love is enduring, and here was a not-so-ordinary man whose conduct demonstrates he knows true love is a process of feeding, keeping, and sharing under all conditions.

What a pleasure it is to witness all along life's paths others—people not driven by tragedy, crisis, or loss—practicing the basic principle of true love. In the usual routines of life, courtesy, consideration, and kindness are often best exhibited in the little day-to-day meaningful expressions that denote real love. I'm thinking of a father I know who takes every appropriate occasion to give his time to his son, sometimes just taking walks and discovering nature's secrets and giving the boy a chance to have his dad all to himself. Think of the mothers you know who have fun teaching their daughters how to bake and cook. There are other mothers who teach their sons to love to read by reading to them and with them. An older brother teaching his younger brother how to start a stamp collection and a sister helping a brother prepare a talk are additional evidences of love in action. We may think "how insignificant, how ordinary," but these and others represent the basics in feeding and, as a result, fun and happiness.

Let me share others: a coach wanting more for his boys than a win; a mother or father willing to stay up until after date time to talk to a daughter or son when the child is in the mood to visit and discuss; a big sister helping a younger sister with her school election campaign plans; a family helping each other get off on a trip. Another evidence of the routine love we appreciate can be found in a college-age girl writing letters of encouragement regularly to a missionary and keeping herself special for marriage to the right young man at the right time in the right place. We also commend the example of fathers who daily teach their children the lesson of true love as they constantly love their wives. Often a helping hand with mundane activities, such as doing the dishes or taking a turn at putting the children to bed, exhibits more true love than sweet expressions made to sound hollow because of inadequate follow-up. Those who truly understand love know that it must be basically simple, continuing, and sincere.

The opportunities for showing love for God through the home, neighborhood, mission field, community, and family are never-ending. Some of us are inclined to terminate our love processes in the family when a member disappoints, rebels, or becomes lost. Sometimes when family members least deserve love, they need it most. Love is not appropriately expressed in threats, accusations, expressions of disappointment, or retaliation. Real love takes time, patience, helping, and continuing performance. I'm thinking of a prospective elder, for more than thirty-five years completely inactive, now feeding me as my home teacher.

"What brought you back, John?" I asked.

"My wife just wouldn't give up on me, and my home teaching companion just kept nudging me in the right way." John is happy and anxiously engaged in the work today because two people in particular know what love is all about.

Love of God takes time. Love of family takes time. Love of country takes time. Love of neighbor takes time. Love of companion takes time. Love in courtship takes time. Love of self takes time.

Whether we are a young son, not wanting to hear of love but preferring to see it in action, a prisoner, a student, a mother, a father, a daughter, or a stranger, we need and deserve more than the declaration, "I love you." Let us resolve to take the time to give of ourselves in putting love into appropriate action and performance. God, too, needs more than words. He is made happy by our feeding, keeping, and continuing.

I pray our Heavenly Father will help us to learn the truth that meaningful love is a continuing process that will bring joy and happiness to all participating parties. May we take the time to show our families, our friends, the stranger, our prophet, and our God that our declarations of love are backed up by performance in our daily lives and that we know that for love to be acceptable to God and man, it must be continuing and originate from within.

Communication Within Our Families

A bewildered father once asked me, "Why is it I seem to be able to communicate with everyone except my own son?"

"What do you mean you can't communicate with your son?" I asked.

"It's just that whenever I try to tell him anything, he tunes me out," he replied.

During our private discussion that followed, and often since, I have concluded that perhaps one of the principal reasons we fail to relate appropriately with family members is because we fail to apply some basics of personal communication. In Hebrews 13:16 we read, "But to do good and to communicate forget not: for with such sacrifices God is well pleased." Communication in the family is often a sacrifice because we are expected to use our time, our means, our talent, and our patience to impart, share, and understand. Too often we use communication periods as occasions to tell, dictate, plead, or threaten. Nowhere in the broadest sense should communication in the family be used to impose, command, or embarrass.

To be effective, family communication must be an exchange of feelings and information. Doors of communication will swing open in the home if members will realize that time and participation on the part of all are necessary ingredients. In family discussions, differences should not be ignored, but should be weighed and evaluated calmly. One's point or opinion usually is not as important as a healthy, continuing relationship. Courtesy and respect in listening and responding during discussions are basic in proper dialogue.

As we learn to participate together in meaningful associations in our families, we are able to convey our thoughts of love, dependence, and interest. When we are inclined to give up in despair in our efforts to communicate because other family members have failed to respond, perhaps we would do well not to give up, but rather to give and take in our conversations. How important it is to know how to disagree with another's point of view without being disagreeable. How important it is to have discussion periods ahead of decisions. Jones Stephens wrote, "I have learned that the head does not hear anything until the heart has listened, and that what the heart knows today the head will understand tomorrow."

Let me share with you seven basic suggestions for more effective family communication.

1. *A willingness to sacrifice.* We must each be the kind of family member who is willing to take time to be available. We need to develop the ability and self-discipline to think of other family members and their communication needs ahead of our own—a willingness to prepare for the moment—the sharing moment, the teaching moment. We need to learn to shed the very appearance of preoccupation in self, and learn the skill of penetrating a family member's shield of preoccupation. Sad is the day when a daughter is heard to say, "My mother gives me everything except herself."

Too early and too often we sow the seeds of "Can't you see I'm busy?" "Don't bother me now." When we convey the attitude of "Go away, don't bother me now," family members are apt to go elsewhere or isolate themselves in silence. All family members on some occasion or other must be taken on their own terms so they will be willing to come, share, and ask.

It takes personal sacrifice to communicate when conditions are right for the other person—during meal preparation, after a date, a hurt, a victory, or a disappointment, or when someone wants to share a confidence. We must be willing to forgo personal convenience to invest time in establishing a firm foundation for family communication. When communication in the family seems to be bogging down, each individual should look to himself for the remedy.

If we would know true love and understanding one for another, we must realize that communication is more than a sharing of words. It is the wise sharing of emotions, feelings, and concerns. It is the sharing of oneself totally. "Who is a wise man and endued with knowledge among you? let him shew out of a good conversation his works with meekness of wisdom." (James 3:13.)

2. *A willingness to set the stage.* The location, setting, or circumstances should be comfortable, private, and conversation-conducive. Effective communications have been shared in a grove of trees, on the mount, by the sea, in family home evening, during a walk, in a car, during a vacation, during a hospital visit, on the way to school, and during the game. When the stage is set, we must be willing to let the other family member be front and center as we appropriately respond.

Months and years after the score of a baseball game is long forgotten, the memory of having been there all alone with Dad will never dim. I'll not soon forget a ten-year-old girl excitedly telling me she had just ridden in the car with her daddy all the way from Salt Lake City to Provo and back. "Was the radio on?" I asked. "Oh, no," she responded, "all Daddy did was listen and talk to me." She had her daddy all to herself in a setting she'll not soon forget. Let the stage be set whenever the need is there. Let the stage be set whenever the other person is ready.

3. *A willingness to listen.* Listening is more than being quiet. Listening is much more than silence. Listening requires undivided attention. The time to listen is when someone needs to be heard. The time to deal with a person with a problem is when he has the problem. The time to listen is the time when our interest and love are vital to the one who seeks our ear, our heart, our help, and our empathy.

We should all increase our ability to ask comfortable questions and then listen—intently, naturally. Listening is a tied-in part of loving. How powerful are the words, "Wherefore, my beloved brethren, let every man be swift to hear, slow to speak, slow to wrath: For the wrath of man worketh not the righteousness of God." (James 1:19-20.)

4. *A willingness to vocalize feelings.* How important it is to be willing to voice one's thoughts and feelings. Yes, how important it is to be able to converse on the level of each family member. Too often we are inclined to let family members assume how we feel toward them. Often wrong conclusions are reached. Often we could have performed better had we known how family members felt about us and what they expected.

How significant are God's words when he vocalized his feelings with, "This is my beloved Son," yes, even the powerful communication, "This is my beloved Son, in whom I am well pleased." (Matthew 3:17.)

Often parents communicate most effectively with their children by the way they listen to and address each other. Their conversations showing gentleness and love are heard by our ever-alert, impressionable children. We must learn to communicate effectively not only by voice, by also by tone, feelings, glances, mannerisms, and total personality. Too often when we are not able to converse with a daughter or wife we wonder, "What is wrong with her?" when we should be wondering, "What is wrong with my methods?" A meaningful smile, an appropriate pat on the shoulder, and a warm handshake are all important. Silence isolates. Strained silent periods cause wonderment, hurt, and, most often, wrong conclusions.

God knows the full impact of continuing communication as he admonishes us to pray constantly. He too has promised to respond as we relate to him effectively.

5. *A willingness to avoid judgment.* If we would improve our communication within our families, we will try to be understanding and not critical. We won't display shock, alarm, or disgust with others' comments or observations. We won't react violently. We will work within the framework of each person's free agency. We will convey the bright, optimistic approach. There is hope. There is a way back. There is a possibility for better understanding.

In our communication, a common ground for personal decision must be developed. "Neither do I condemn thee: go, and sin no more" (John 8:11) are words that are just as gentle and effective today as when they were first uttered.

We must avoid imposing our values on others. When we can learn to deal with issues without involving personalities, and at the same time avoid bias and emotions, we are on our way to effective family communication. When a family member makes a decision that may be inadequate or improper, do we have the ability and patience to convey the attitude that we don't agree with his decision but he has the right of choice and is still a loved member of the family?

It is easy to point out mistakes and pass judgment. Sincere compliments and praise come much harder from most of us. It takes real maturity for a parent to apologize to a child for an error. An honest apology often makes the son or daughter feel surprisingly warm toward the mother or father or brother or sister. "For in many things we offend all. If any man offend not in word, the same is a perfect man, and able also to bridle the whole body." (James 3:2.)

6. *A willingness to maintain confidences.* We must be worthy of trust even in trivial questions and observations. Weighty questions and observations will follow only if we have been trustworthy with the trivial. In all our communications we should treat innermost trusts and concerns with respect and build on deserved trust. Individuals who are blessed to have a relationship with someone to whom they can confidently talk and trust are fortunate indeed. Who is to say a family trust is not greater than a community trust?

7. *A willingness to practice patience.* Patience in communication is that certain ingredient of conduct we hope others will exhibit toward us when we fail to measure up. Our own patience is developed when we are patient with others. The Lord has told us, "Be patient; be sober; be temperate; have patience, faith, hope and charity." (D&C 6:19.)

"I get sick and tired of listening to your complaints" and "I have told you a thousand times" are but two of many often-repeated family quotations that indicate patience is gone and channels of communication are plugged.

It takes courage to communicate patiently. We need to constantly express pride, hope, and love on a most sincere basis. Each of us needs to avoid coming through as one who has given up and has become totally weary in trying.

The correction of family members in front of others is to be avoided. Much more notice is taken in quiet, private conversation. Calm endurance is a priceless virtue in one's relationship with all family members.

When family members tune each other out, communication is not taking place. Words spoken are

unheard, unwanted, and resisted when we fail to understand the basics for proper interchange. Each must be
willing to do his part to improve, since the family unit is
the basic foundation of the Church. Proper communication will always be a main ingredient for building family
solidarity and permanence.

I pray our Heavenly Father will help us to communicate more effectively in the home through a willingness
to sacrifice, a willingness to listen, a willingness to vocalize feelings, a willingness to avoid judgment, a willingness to maintain confidences, and a willingness to
practice patience. "How forcible are right words!" (Job
6:25.) Yes, how forcible are right words shared at the
right moment with the right person.

No Time for Contention

A few months ago word reached some of our missionaries on a remote South Pacific island that I would soon be visiting there for two or three days. When I arrived, the missionaries were waiting anxiously to share with me some anti-Mormon literature that was being circulated in their area. They were disturbed by the accusations and were eager to plan retaliation.

The elders sat on the edge of their chairs as I read the slander and false declarations issued by a minister who apparently felt threatened by their presence and success. As I read the pamphet containing the malicious and ridiculous statements, I actually smiled, much to the surprise of my young associates. When I finished, they asked, "What do we do now? How can we best counteract such lies?"

I answered, "To the author of these words, we do nothing. We have no time for contention. We only have time to be about our Father's business. Contend with no man. Conduct yourselves as gentlemen with calmness and conviction, and I promise you success."

Perhaps a formula for these missionaries and all of us to follow can be found in the Book of Mormon: "And it came to pass when they heard this voice, and beheld that it was not a voice of thunder, neither was it a voice of a great tumultuous noise, but behold, it was a still voice of perfect mildness, as if it had been a whisper, and it did pierce even to the very soul." (Helaman 5:30.)

There never has been a time when it is more important for us as members of The Church of Jesus Christ of Latter-day Saints to take a stand, remain firm in our convictions, and conduct ourselves wisely under all circumstances. We must not be manipulated or enraged by those who subtly foster contention over issues of the day.

When issues are in contradiction to the laws of God, the Church must take a stand and state its position. We have done this in the past and will continue to do so in the future when basic moral principles are attacked. There are those in our society who would promote misconduct and immoral programs for financial gain and popularity. When others disagree with our stand we should not argue, retaliate in kind, or contend with them. We can maintain proper relationships and avoid the frustrations of strife if we wisely apply our time and energies.

Ours is to conscientiously avoid being abrasive in our presentations and declarations. We need constantly to remind ourselves that when we are unable to change the conduct of others, we will go about the task of properly governing ourselves.

Certain people and organizations are trying to provoke us into contention with slander, innuendos, and improper classifications. How unwise we are in today's society to allow ourselves to become irritated, dismayed, or offended because others seem to enjoy the role of misstating our position or involvement. Our principles or standards will not be less than they are because of the statements of the contentious.

Ours is to explain our position through reason, friendly persuasion, and accurate facts. Ours is to stand firm and unyielding on the moral issues of the day and the eternal principles of the gospel, but to contend with no man or organization. Contention builds walls and puts up barriers. Love opens doors. Ours is to be heard and to teach. Ours is not only to avoid contention, but also to see that such things are done away.

"For verily, verily I say unto you, he that hath the spirit of contention is not of me, but is of the devil, who is the father of contention, and he stirreth up the hearts of men to contend with anger, one with another.

"Behold, this is not my doctrine, to stir up the hearts of men with anger, one against another; but this is my doctrine, that such things should be done away." (3 Nephi 11:29-30.)

We need to be reminded that contention is a striving against one another, especially in controversy or argument. It is to struggle, fight, battle, quarrel, or dispute. Contention never was and never will be an ally of progress. Our loyalty will never be measured by our participation in controversy.

Some misunderstand the realm, scope, and angers of contention. Too many of us are inclined to declare, "Who, me? I am not contentious, and I'll fight anyone who says I am." There are still those among us who would rather lose a friend than an argument. How important it is to know how to disagree without being disagreeable. It behooves all of us to be in the position to involve ourselves in factual discussions and meaningful study, but never in bitter arguments and contention.

No home or heart exists that cannot be hurt through contention. It is sad when children are raised in a contentious home. It is just as sad when an organization has contention as one of the planks of its platform, declared or unannounced. Generally speaking, people who come from noncontentious households find themselves repulsed by those who make it part of the daily diet.

The family as an institution today is beset on all sides. Conflicts within the family are critical and often damaging. Contention puts heavy strain on stability, strength, peace, and unity in the home. There is certainly not time for contention in building a strong family.

In place of arguments and friction between family members, ours is to build, listen, and reason together. I recall receiving a written question from a fifteen-year-old girl during a fireside discussion. She wrote, "Is there anything I can do to improve the feelings among members of my family? I am fifteen years old and hardly ever look forward to being home. Everyone just seems to be waiting for me to say the wrong thing so they can cut me down."

Another young woman, age seventeen, was asked why she was living with her sister in a city away from their parents. She replied, "Because of the hassle back home. I have had all that I can stand. There is always fighting. I can never remember when it was different. Everyone in the house, especially my parents, takes delight in bad mouthing each other."

A few family expressions that cause hurts and lead to contention are: "You don't know what you're talking about." "Why did you do such a stupid thing?" "Your room is a mess." "Why don't you do as I tell you?"

Almost five centuries ago a creative genius named Leonardo da Vinci lived and worked in Italy. While we remember him most today for such paintings as the *Mona Lisa,* he was also a fascinating debater, a polished orator, and a storyteller of great imagination. One of his fables was simply titled "The Wolf." Da Vinci wrote:

"Carefully, warily, the wolf came down out of the forest one night, attracted by the smell of a flock of sheep. With slow steps he drew near to the sheepfold, placing his feet with the utmost caution so as not to make the slightest sound which might disturb the sleeping dog.

"But one careless paw stepped on a board; the board creaked and woke the dog. The wolf had to run away, unfed and hungry. And so, because of one careless foot, the whole animal suffered."

There is an area, perhaps insignificant to some, that seems to me to be gnawing away at the spirituality of Latter-day Saints. The plights of the two young women bring it to mind. Like the careless paw of the wolf, it is causing untold suffering and depriving many of spiritual growth and family oneness. I speak of arguing, careless words spoken in anger, disgust, and intolerance, often without thought. How sad it is when family members are driven from home by contentious tongues.

Stories often reiterate the hate and bitterness caused by contention among neighbors. Some families have been forced to move because of bitter controversy. Going the extra mile, turning the other cheek, swallowing one's pride, and apologizing are often the only ways in which contention among neighbors can be erased.

From the Savior's words we learn the source of contention, whether it be in the home, in the community, among leaders, or in the classroom. "For verily, verily, I say unto you, he that hath the spirit of contention is not of me, but is of the devil, who is the father of contention, and he stirreth up the hearts of men to contend with anger, one with another." (3 Nephi 11:29.)

This means that Satan has power over us only when we let him in. We have agency. We can choose our behavior. The Prophet Joseph Smith said on one occasion, "The devil has no power over us only as we permit him. The moment we revolt at anything which comes from God, the devil takes power." (*Teachings of the Prophet Joseph Smith,* p. 181.)

When one considers the bad feelings and the unpleasantness caused by contention, it is well to ask, "Why do I participate?" If we are really honest with ourselves, our answers may be similar to these: "When I argue and am disagreeable, I do not have to change myself. It gives me a chance to get even." "I am unhappy and I want others to be miserable too." "I can feel self-righteous. In this way I get my ego built up." "I don't want others to forget how much I know."

Whatever the real reason, it is important to recognize that we choose our behavior. At the root of this issue is the age-old problem of pride. "Only by pride cometh contention." (Proverbs 13:10.)

If Satan can succeed in creating in us habits of arguing, quarreling, and contention, it is easier then for him to bind us with the heavier sins that can destroy our eternal lives. A contentious spirit can affect almost any phase of our lives. An angry letter written in haste can haunt us sometimes for years. A few ill-advised words spoken in hate can destroy a marriage or a personal friendship or impede community progress.

As we take a stand against the evils of the day, such as abortion, homosexuality, immorality, alcohol, drugs, dishonesty, and intolerance, can we express our beliefs without clenching our fists, raising our voices, and promoting contention?

Can we talk about the beneficial principles of the gospel, such as the Word of Wisdom, keeping the Sabbath day holy, maintaining personal purity, and the other truths found in the scriptures, without making our listeners defensive?

This is not easy, but it can be done. Ours is, if you please, to plow our own furrow, plant our own seeds, tend our crops, and reap the harvest. This can best be accomplished not only by plowshares rather than by swords, but also by appropriate commitment rather than contention.

Here are some suggestions for alleviating contention:

1. We need to pray to have the love of God in our hearts. Sometimes this is a struggle, but the Spirit of the Lord can soften hard feelings and mellow a callous spirit.

2. We need to learn to control our tongues. An old

maxim says, "Think twice before you speak and three times before you act."

3. We need to avoid allowing emotions to take over; rather, we should reason together.

4. We need to refuse to get embroiled in the same old patterns of argument and confrontation.

5. We need to practice speaking in a soft, calm voice. The peaceful life can best be attained not by those who speak with a voice of "great tumultuous noise," but by those who follow the Savior's example and speak with "a still voice of perfect mildness." (Helaman 5:30.)

There is no time for contention. We must have the will and discipline in our daily lives to fight contention. The valiant can have the help of our Father in their efforts to conquer this horrendous foe. Let us "cease to contend one with another; cease to speak evil one of another." (D&C 136:23.) We only have time to be about our Father's business.

"Come In Without Knocking"

A few years ago I had a small sign made and placed on a door in one of my offices. It read, "Come in without knocking and leave the same way." It was interesting to observe people's expressions as they pondered this play on words. According to the dictionary, knock has two definitions: "to strike something with a sharp blow" and "to find fault with, a harsh and often petty criticism." Perhaps in human relationships both of these meanings could apply. This sign served as a reminder to me to come into the office without finding fault and to leave at the close of the day the same way. It was also our hope that it might help others who entered and left.

There is a tendency among too many in our society today, young and old, to knock the establishment, knock the community, and knock the neighbors. There is a certain growing segment of society that would rather knock than kneel, rather knock than negotiate, rather knock than know. They have left unheeded the truth found in Psalms: "This is the day which the Lord hath made; we will rejoice and be glad in it." (Psalm 118:24.)

There is a great need today for all mankind to heed the plea to cease to find fault one with another. Some of us are so accustomed to wearing faultfinding spectacles that we cannot see past them. We need to open our eyes and ears and look for the good and the blessings around us. The apostle Paul wrote: "Eye hath not seen, nor ear heard, neither have entered into the heart of men, the things which God hath prepared for them that love him." (1 Corinthians 2:9.)

If we love God, we will love our fellowmen. If we love God, we will appreciate and acknowledge his wondrous creations.

It was disturbing as well as alarming to read the comments of some youths who were asked, "If you were to write a letter to someone on another planet, what would you tell them to convince them to either come to earth or stay away?" They responded: "Stay where you are because you can't breathe here and you'll get beat up in the streets." "Stay away. Earth is already too crowded and too polluted." "Stay away. Humans are narrow-minded people who couldn't accept you as you are and the world is such a mess you probably wouldn't live because of our polluted environment." "Stay away. There is nothing for anyone here except trouble."

Comments such as these remind us of the universal need to take heed of the admonition of Paul: "Finally, brethren, whatsoever things are true, whatsoever things are honest, whatsoever things are pure, whatsoever things are lovely, whatsoever things are of good report; if there be any virtue, if there be any praise, think on these things." (Philippians 4:8.)

We sometimes unknowingly find fault with God when we ignore or criticize his children. God loves us. He will make our paths bright and joyous as we come to know him and his eternal ways. Faultfinding is a great deterrent to man's progress. A worthy daily prayer might well be for us to ask our Heavenly Father for the strength and determination to cease finding fault one with another. Almost all persons will respond to sincere praise and rebel at harsh and cutting criticisms.

Let me share with you the positive, progressive attitude of a friend of mine who had been confined in the

Utah State Prison. "I don't want to blame anyone back home for my being in prison, but it is factual that I had no family relationships. I was involved in the family home evening program at the prison. Without the people who were assigned to me through this program, many times I would have given up. These people loved me as if I were their own son. I have never had that, even when I was a small boy. Now with their help and the help of others I believe I can make it back a day at a time. I am not proud of having been in prison, but I am proud of my recent experiences there. We have a tendency to blame others. We don't want to blame our parents for not loving us, because we know they do, but maybe they didn't have the guidance and direction in their lives to apply when they were bringing us up."

Perhaps in the minds of many this fine young man would be justified in knocking his parents, society, and our systems, but he didn't. Instead, he is thanking those who have helped him and is sincerely grateful for the direction in which his life is moving today.

Church attenders in prisons are, unfortunately, in the minority and are often classified by their associates in uncomplimentary terms, but this fine young man is not ashamed to be identified as a member of "God's Squad."

We are living in a day when we need to look for the good in neighbors, associates, and family members. It is hard for any one of us to find heroes among our neighbors when our pleasures seem wrapped up in faultfinding. Probably the greatest discovery for mankind can be found in ordinary neighbors. We generally find that for which we are looking. We need to speak the good word, build our associates, and cease finding fault. We need to thank God for life, opportunities, and his love.

I once visited with an elder in the mission field and asked him, "Is your father a member of the Church?"

77

"No."

"Is your mother a member?"

"Just barely."

"Did your father want you to go on a mission?"

"No."

"Did your mother want you to go on a mission?"

"She really didn't care whether I went or not."

"Who influenced you most in your decision to go?"

"I did. I've always wanted to go and I knew I could make a success of it."

I looked at that young man and said, "From what I hear and what I feel of your spirit, you will succeed." Here was a great individual who had the opportunity to knock and to murmur, "My dad doesn't care. My mother doesn't care. Why should I care?" But he knew the importance of going forward and had the courage to continue.

Wouldn't it be wonderful if every neighborhood fence, every office, every home, every church, every club house, every classroom, yes, every telephone, could be labeled, "Come in without knocking and leave the same way."

May we realize it is our challenge to be doers of the word, not critics, not those who murmur or are self-indulging faultfinders. Blessings lie in store for those who will cease finding fault one with another and will truly love God, neighbors, and family members. We cannot walk in truth by stepping on others. If we will live together in love, we will cease faultfinding, and will come and go without knocking.

Murmur Not

The dictionary defines the word *murmur* as "a half-suppressed or muttered complaint; grumbling; a low, indistinct, but often continuous sound; an atypical sound of the heart indicating a functional or structural abnormality."

May I, in the spirit of that definition, be brave enough to suggest that perhaps people who are prone to complain on a continuous basis are functionally or structurally abnormal? Some intellectually inclined and some not so intellectually inclined citizens tend to sit back and murmur, forgetting that there is a manly right and privilege to meet issues and questions openly. How shabby is he who would rather murmur than know.

Some time ago I noticed a friend of mine was very skilled and very able at murmuring. In fact, I think she was the most skilled murmurer I have ever heard. She was a professional. When she murmured everyone listened because it was always juicy and alarming. So I asked my friend, "How would you like to accept a challenge?"

"What is it?"

"How would you like to try to go two weeks without murmuring or gossiping or backbiting or finding fault?"

She ducked her head a little bit and then said, "Well, if you want, I'll try it."

After the two weeks were over she looked me up and, in response to my question, "Did you make it?" she said, "I did. It wasn't easy but I did make it." Then she added, "And I want you to know it was the dullest two weeks of my life!"

It may be an interesting pastime for some of us to murmur, but I want to tell you it is a dangerous habit. One of my young friends, after completing the reading of the Book of Mormon for the first time, and being impressed with what he had read about Laman and Lemuel, said to me, "What do you think was the primary difference between Laman and Lemuel and their brother Nephi when it came to performance and achievement in the great activities of that day?"

Without hesitation I said, "The difference between Laman and Lemuel and Nephi was the fact that Laman and Lemuel were inclined to murmur, find fault, and whisper under their breaths—not always in a whisper— their displeasure with everything going on." Laman and Lemuel were not as trusted or as successful as Nephi because they were in very deed inclined to murmur. Nephi wrote:

"Now this he [Lehi] spake because of the stiffneckedness of Laman and Lemuel; for behold they did murmur in many things against their father, because he was a visionary man, and had led them out of the land of Jerusalem, to leave the land of their inheritance, and their gold, and their silver, and their precious things, to perish in the wilderness. And this they said he had done because of the foolish imaginations of his heart.

"And thus Laman and Lemuel, being the eldest, did murmur against their father. And they did murmur because they knew not the dealings of that God who had created them." (1 Nephi 2:11-12.)

Later Lehi spoke to Nephi, saying:

"And now, behold thy brothers murmur, saying it is a hard thing which I have required of them; but behold

I have not required it of them, but it is a commandment of the Lord.

"Therefore go, my son, and thou shalt be favored of the Lord, because thou hast not murmured." (1 Nephi 3:6.)

Even Father Lehi on a day of discouragement murmured against the Lord and was rebuked. "And it came to pass that the voice of the Lord came unto my father; and he was truly chastened because of his murmuring against the Lord, insomuch that he was brought down into the depths of sorrow." (1 Nephi 16:25.)

Nephi was blessed with the courage and wisdom to murmur not. He had neither the time nor the inclination to murmur. Life was full. Life was challenging. Life was rewarding. He constantly encouraged his associates, including his brothers, to participate diligently in the work of the Lord and shun the business of murmuring.

I am reminded of an experience in the life of Emma Smith, the wife of the Prophet, who was inclined on occasion to murmur. I think we could accurately say that on occasion Emma wanted to be where the action was. She wanted to know what was going on. She wanted to be a party to the translation. She wanted to see the records. And so Emma murmured because she was left out. This prompted the Lord to give us section 25 of the Doctrine and Covenants, in which she was instructed:

"Murmur not because of the things which thou hast not seen, for they are withheld from thee and from the world, which is wisdom in me in a time to come.

"And the office of thy calling shall be for a comfort unto my servant, Joseph Smith, Jun., thy husband, in his afflictions, with consoling words, in the spirit of meekness. . . .

"Continue in the spirit of meekness, and beware of pride. Let thy soul delight in thy husband, and the glory which shall come upon him." (D&C 25:4-5, 14.)

Our challenges today are to serve where we are called

and to serve without murmur and to serve without reservation. The stouthearted do not have time to murmur.

Some time ago I had an experience that taught me firsthand the importance of not murmuring or complaining in a situation when we might think we have every reason to do so.

Returning from an assignment in the Los Angeles area, I boarded a plane and took the only remaining seat on the aisle, front row, in the nonsmoking section. I sat down, fastened my belt, and the plane was soon taxiing out for takeoff. After we had reached a certain altitude, the no-smoking sign went off, and the woman next to me opened her purse, took out a cigarette, and lit it. I looked at her and then at the sign overhead that said, "No-smoking Section." Immediately the thought came to me, "Perhaps I could nudge her and say, 'Can't you read? Can't you see where you are?'" Then, on second thought, I decided that perhaps she was nervous and thought she needed that cigarette, so I allowed her to finish it and hoped that would be the end. But as soon as that was out, she lit another one. While I was trying to read and appear not to be too disturbed, I was boiling just a bit because my rights and privileges were being abused. This continued until we arrived in Salt Lake City.

Finally, as we were making an approach to land in Salt Lake City, she leaned over to me and said, "I hope we have a soft landing."

"Any particular reason why you would like us to have a soft landing?" I asked.

She said, "Yes, under the seat I have some china items that I am bringing to Salt Lake City for my daughter. She is being married tomorrow."

"Where is your daughter being married?"

"In the Mormon Tabernacle."

"Oh. And are you going to the Mormon Tabernacle to see your daughter married?"

"No, I can't go to the Mormon Tabernacle because I am not a member of the Mormon Church."

"How long has your daughter been a member of the Church?"

"About two years. She was attending the University of Utah and became acquainted with the Church and was baptized about two years ago."

"And who is your daughter marrying?"

"A returned Mormon minister."

About this time we landed, the plane came to a stop, and the door was opened for our departure. As we made our way down the steps and into the waiting area, two good-looking young people, a handsome young man and a beautiful young woman, ran up. The girl greeted her mother with open arms and hugged her. Then she looked past her mother, saw me, and said, "Oh, Mother, I would like you to meet Elder Ashton, one of the apostles of our church." About then the thought crossed my mind, "Why, I had the right to nudge her and say, 'Can't you see? Can't you read? Can't you understand you're violating my rights?' " I really appreciate the fact that for once I was tolerant and able to learn and understand from a person who sat next to me—someone whom I could possibly have abused verbally because I had the right to.

As we walked out of the terminal together, just the four of us—the mother, the daughter, the prospective son-in-law, and I—I said to this young couple, "Congratulations on being married in the Mormon Tabernacle." The girl smiled and said, "Who told you that?"

"Your mom."

She said, "Mom, you misunderstood. I'm being married in the temple."

Her mother said, "What's the difference?" For the next three or four minutes I heard a daughter tell her mother the difference between a tabernacle marriage and a temple marriage. How proud I was of her, the way she was able to explain to her mother where she was being married, not on the tabernacle grounds, but in the temple for time and all eternity. I walked out very pleased for that experience of having an opportunity to learn and possibly teach tolerance and patience and also the importance of holding my tongue and murmuring not.

May I share with you another experience to illustrate the rewards of one who did not take the occasion or the time to murmur. Some time ago I was in a stake conference. When it was time for the closing prayer, the stake president announced the name of the individual who had been given the assignment. There were four verses in the closing hymn. At the beginning of the third verse I noticed a young man in the audience start to make his way to the pulpit to give the prayer. As he came toward the pulpit I noticed he was moving with a great deal of difficulty, and as he came even closer I saw that one leg was heavily braced. He walked slowly, with a cane. He barely made it to the pulpit before the song was over.

After the benediction, the stake president nudged me and said, "This young man has just returned from the mission field. About two and one-half years ago he came to me after visiting with his bishop and said, "I'd like to go on a mission. I know I have physical handicaps but I would like to go." The stake president hesitated, wondering what to say to the young man. Finally the young man said, to press the point, "President, if you and the bishop will let me go on a mission, I promise you one thing." The stake president said, "What is it?" He said, "I promise you if you'll let me go, I'll never get in anyone's way."

He went on his mission and he served honorably in the West Central States Mission, where he had the opportunity of baptizing forty-seven people—a great individual who had the right, we might say, to murmur, find fault with his God, find fault with his parents, find fault with the community, but he was stouthearted. He didn't have the time nor the inclination to murmur.

This is a day when we need dedicated Latter-day Saints bearing testimony of the truthfulness of the gospel. We don't need those who would lurk in the dark shadows and murmur. We need those who will stand by our prophet, sustain him, support him, and perform for him. We need those who will not make slighting remarks about their bishop or second-guess their stake president or criticize their home teachers. Instead of these don'ts, let us be builders and build ourselves as we build others.

There are those in our society who murmur against God. There are those who murmur against this great country. There are those who murmur against their friends. There are even those who murmur against the Church.

"Cease to contend one with another; cease to speak evil one of another." (D&C 136:23.)

If we have associates who are inclined to murmur, I hope and pray that we will help them overcome this habit and find their way back. In my mind, the reason Oliver Cowdery, David Whitmer, and Martin Harris fell away after having the divine revelations and experiences that they had is primarily because they were inclined to murmur. I also think that the Prophet Joseph Smith had great difficulty, trials and tribulations, and physical harm bestowed upon him because many of his close associates were inclined to murmur instead of to stand by and support him.

The adversary has no stronger weapon in his possession for the downfall of our Heavenly Father's children or institutions than murmuring. This is our Heavenly Father's work. This is his kingdom. We have been blessed with gifts and abilities. We have assignments and charges, but we do not have the right when we are unhappy with ourselves or with conditions to murmur against God, leaders, or companions. Our challenge in this direction is to live lives of true Latter-day Saints, with dignity and with pride.

He Answered Nothing

Jesus stood before the governor: and the governor asked him, Art thou the King of the Jews? And Jesus said unto them, Thou sayest.

"And when he was accused of the chief priests and elders, he answered nothing.

"Then said Pilate unto him, Hearest thou not how many things they witness against thee?

"And he answered him to never a word." (Matthew 27:11-14.)

Sometimes the most effective sermons are delivered in silence. Sometimes the most convincing messages are delivered in silence. Often the sweetest tones are rendered in silence. And sometimes the most penetrating responses are presented in silence. I think that it is significant that Jesus said, "He that hath seen me hath seen the Father" rather than saying, "If you have heard me you have heard the Father." (See John 14:9.) His example bore witness; his life was a sermon.

There are times when muscle tone, mental tone, emotional tone, and spiritual tone can most effectively speak for themselves in silence. The following are some sermons I will not soon forget. All of them were taught in silence.

Some years ago I had the opportunity of witnessing a state championship high school track meet at Brigham

Young University. The lesson I learned as I watched the mile run was most impressive. About a dozen young men had qualified to represent their schools. The gun was fired, and these young men who had trained so long and so hard took off. Four fellows, closely bunched together, took the lead. Suddenly the runner in second place spiked the first runner's foot with his shoe. As the leader was about to make the next stride forward, he found that he was without a shoe.

As I noticed this, I wondered what the leader would do because of what his competitor had unintentionally done to him. It seemed to me he had a number of choices. He could take a few extra quick sprints and catch up to the fellow who had put him out of first position, double up his fist, and hit him to get even. He could run over to the coach and say, "This is what you get—I have trained all my life for this big day, and now look what's happened!" He could run off into the stands and say to his mother and father, "See what happened?" Or he could have sat down on the track and cried. But to my pleasure, he did not do any of these things. He just kept running.

This was halfway around the first lap, and I thought to myself, "Good for him; he'll finish this first lap of the four and retire gracefully." But after he had completed the first lap, he just kept running. He completed the second lap, then the third lap—and everytime he took a stride, cinders were coming up through his stocking. But he kept running, and when he was through, he had said nothing. I thought, "What parents! What a coach! What leaders who have affected his life enough so that in a situation like this he would say nothing!" He finished the job he had to do. He did not place first, but he was a real winner.

On another occasion I sat at a basketball game watching Brigham Young University's team. Before the game there were catcalls. There were threats. There were accusations. There were pending protests. There were possible violences against Coach Stan Watts and his team. As I sat there in the stands and listened, and even watched as obstacles were thrown on the court, the question came to my mind, "What will Stan do, what will he say?" Stan Watts said nothing. He led his players on to the floor. They came, they stayed, and they performed without saying a word. He led his men and he taught us a lesson.

Several years ago I had the opportunity of playing tennis with my very close friend, Dr. Joseph S. Wood, a popular instructor at Brigham Young University. Early in the game he came to me and said, "Let me rest just a moment; I am getting dizzy." So I stood and waited, and he remained in difficulty. I suggested that he sit down, and he did. Then I asked him to stretch himself out on the court to see if the dizziness would leave him. After a few minutes, realizing the strain and possible seriousness of the situation, I asked him to stand and go with me to the car so we could get medical attention. To my shock, he could not walk; his right arm and leg would not respond. He also could not talk. I got some help and we carried him from the court to the car and to a doctor.

That evening after Brother Wood was taken to the hospital, his wife, Jan, asked us to come and administer to him. After the administration I looked down at Joe and said, "How are you doing?" He said nothing, but he gripped my arm with his left hand. As I looked into his eyes, I saw determination. I read the message, "I'll come back. I can make it." I learned a great lesson that night. Joe did come back. Within a few months he was walking, riding, speaking, and going forward in a manner in which we who know him best had confidence he would. He had silently told us he would.

One weekend I had the opportunity of attending stake quarterly conference in Gooding, Idaho. As a group of Primary children stood before the congregation and sang "I Am a Child of God," I noticed three young Primary members on the front row singing but saying nothing vocally. They were deaf; they sang with their hands. No one heard them audibly—because they said nothing—but we received their message. They touched my spirit deeply, and it was my privilege to tell them in front of the members of that stake that our Heavenly Father heard them. Even though vocally they had said nothing, they transmitted a memorable message. In moving silence they taught of the spirit, they taught of the mind, and they taught of the heart.

Another friend that I hope we can learn from is a man I have never met, but I feel that I know him. Some years ago we were in Suva, Fiji, on Church assignment. As we were checking in at the Grand Palace Hotel, I noticed opposite from the registration desk a painting. I was so taken with it that I walked over to it to learn the name of the painter. There was a little word of explanation in the corner. It read something like this: "This painting is by Semesi Mayo, leading artist, a leper. With no fingers or hands he painted this scene with the use of his toes, his feet, and his mouth." This is Fiji's leading artist, and no one sees him because he is confined and restricted as to where he may live. I felt that day that I knew him. He had said nothing; he was not even seen, but his works and his message were.

A few years ago Peter Snell of New Zealand was the ultimate in the world in the one-mile race and the 880-yard race. We had the opportunity of meeting him in Wellington. Later on in the week someone said to me, "Would you like to see where Peter Snell does his training and his running?" I answered yes. I was shocked when I was taken down to the beach—not to a track but to the beach. I asked, "Where does he run?" My friends said, "He runs out close to the water where the sand comes up over his feet. There it is difficult to pull his feet out after each stride." I had an idea why, but I said to my friends, "Why does he run there?" They answered, "When he gets on a track in competition, he feels like he's floating, because he doesn't have to pull his feet up out of the wet sand."

In my mind I could see him running on that difficult track. He said nothing to me then, but I saw him, and I learned from him. A little later my friends took me to another place where Peter Snell trained up in the mountains. When I looked for a track again, they said, "No, he runs up the steep hills. Then, when he is on the level at track meets, it is pretty easy to run." That is why he breaks records, and that is why I remember him even though he has said nothing to me since I saw his training grounds.

May we so live that others, when observing us in our silence, say, "He answered nothing, but he touches my heart and lifts my mind because of what he is."

He Listens

The first word of the first verse of the first section of the Doctrine and Covenants is *listen*. Twenty-five other sections of the Doctrine and Covenants start out with the word *listen* or *hearken*. The first words God said to young Joseph Smith in the glorious vision when the Father and the Son appeared to him were, "*This is My Beloved Son. Hear Him!*" (Joseph Smith—History 1:17.) He was saying, in essence, "Joseph, you have come here seeking information and counsel and direction. Now listen and you will be instructed." What is more important than hearkening and listening? Joseph Smith revealed the will of God because he was willing to listen.

Isn't it also significant that God listens? That's why he heard Joseph's prayer. That's why he appeared with his Son. Do you think God would say to us, "Pray constantly that you may not be led into temptation," if he weren't going to listen? God does listen. He hears and he answers.

Would it then be unreasonable to suggest that perhaps some of our prayers are not answered because we don't take the time to listen? Would it be out of place to recommend that perhaps in a large percent of our prayers we should be listening instead of placing orders and making requests and saying in an indirect way, "Lord, I've mentioned this to you before. Where are you?" I think sometimes he would say, "Where are you? I'd like to talk to you."

I like to think of the quotation, ". . . how often would I have gathered thy children together, even as a hen gathereth her chickens under her wings, and ye would not!" (Matthew 23:37.) I would just like to add one word to the end of that verse: "You would not *listen*." "He that hath ears to hear, let him hear." (Matthew 11:15.) "Wherefore, my beloved brethren, let every man be swift to hear, slow to speak. . . ." (James 1:19.)

Why did Jesus of Nazareth ask questions in his teachings? So he could listen and analyze the thinking processes of the individual or individuals confronted. One of the great joys of temple work, one of the great joys of genealogical work is the occasion and the environment in which we can properly listen.

There is an Indian proverb I enjoy: "Listen or thy tongue will keep thee deaf." I have had to say to young people many times, "God will answer your prayers, he will hear you, if you'll take the time to listen and not become impatient."

May I refer to one powerful scripture as it relates to listening and silence:

"And the scribes and Pharisees brought unto him [Jesus] a woman taken in adultery; and when they had set her in the midst,

"They say unto him, Master, this woman was taken in adultery, in the very act.

"Now Moses in the law commanded us, that such should be stoned: but what sayest thou?

"This they said, tempting him, that they might have to accuse him. But Jesus stooped down, and with his finger wrote on the ground, as though he heard them not.

"So when they continued asking him, he lifted up himself, and said unto them, He that is without sin among you, let him first cast a stone at her.

94

"And again he stooped down, and wrote on the ground."

We don't know what the Savior wrote, but I like to think the writing on the ground was just a pause to give those who had gathered to confuse and condemn him a chance to listen to his spirit, to his power, with nothing being said.

"And they which heard it, being convicted by their own conscience, went out one by one, beginning at the eldest, even unto the last; and Jesus was left alone, and the woman standing in the midst.

"When Jesus had lifted up himself and saw none but the woman, he said unto her, Woman, where are those thine accusers? hath no man condemned thee?

"She said, No man, Lord. And Jesus said unto her, Neither do I condemn thee: go, and sin no more." (John 8:3-11.)

Let's look now at some modern-day examples of the joys and blessings of listening if we will communicate with, confer with, and understand our associates.

A middle-aged woman came to see me at the recommendation of her bishop and stake president. We had a one-hour interview over some very serious problems in her life. In the first forty-five minutes I said about twenty words. In the next fifteen minutes I said a little more. I'll never forget the woman's remarks when she left me: "Brother Ashton, you'll never know how wonderful it's been to have you talk to me." I think that's the kind of talk most of us like—when someone will listen to us and not just sit and be silent; when someone will actually hear us and show us that they are concerned with our problems and will take the time to be, hopefully, a party to the solution.

One day as I was leaving the Utah State Prison following some meetings there, an inmate grabbed me by the arm and said, "Could I talk to you for a moment?" I was in a hurry to get somewhere else, but I stopped for about fifteen minutes, and I listened and I listened. When I left, this big, rugged, tough guy merely said, "Thank you, Mr. Ashton, for talking to me." I don't think I said anything except "What else?" or "tell me more."

In Tahiti, where we were organizing a new stake, I met a young man twenty-six years of age, who had been a member of the Church for one year. He asked, "May I see you for a moment after the meeting? I have a problem. I'd just like a few moments of your time." When the meeting was over we stepped aside privately and I said, "All right, tell me about your problem." I found out he came from a well-to-do family of French extraction. He said, "My parents were wealthy enough to give me a good education in Paris. I have a degree in brewing. I am the only person here on the island who has the knowledge and skill of brewing." He had had a course in the proper way, if there is such a way, of brewing alcoholic beverages. That was his education. Then he said, "I'm a member of the Church now, and I want to know what I should do about my profession."

As I thought about his question, I decided it might be a good idea to listen. So I asked him, "How do you feel about it?" "I don't feel very good about it." "What's your problem?" "I have a conflict." "What do you intend to do about your conflict?" He replied, "I intend to give up my profession." "Any more questions?" I asked. In five minutes he had answered his own question. His problem was bothering him, and he wanted to do something about it. He will do something about it.

Will you take the time to listen when you're confronted by family or friends? Or will you want to do the talking?

We don't always have to have perfect hearing ability physically to be good listeners. Some people who have perfect physical facilities for hearing never hear. Some people born physically deaf are among our greatest listeners.

I bear witness that God listens. He hears and he hearkens to our prayers when we're in tune and pray with faith unwavering, and with contrite hearts and spirits. There is a great blessing in respectful, quiet listening. It helps us to know God.

Appreciation—A Sign of Maturity

Appreciation for people and events that come into our lives is most important because it is God's way of helping us to grow. The ultimate maturity is being able to feel and express appreciation, being fully aware of value and importance, and showing gratitude for it. How does God feel about appreciation? In the Doctrine and Covenants we read: "And in nothing doth man offend God, or against none is his wrath kindled, save those who confess not his hand in all things, and obey not his commandments." (D&C 59:21.)

Would you like to have God's wrath raised against you? Would you like to have God mad at you? It can come and it will happen if we fail to show appreciation and gratitude. Why does the lack of appreciation offend God and kindle his wrath? Not because he needs to see and hear our appreciation and gratitude, but because he knows an absence of appreciation on the part of anyone causes personal stagnation. Our growth and our progress are delayed when we fail to feel and express our appreciation. May we think for a few moments about occasions and situations where we actually say, "Thank thee, God, for people and events that have come into our lives that have made it possible for us to develop and grow and mature, for all people, for all conditions, and for all circumstances that allow us to appreciate human beings and situations for what they can do and will mean to us."

As we visit with missionaries, we often ask them to stand up and tell us where they are from, bear their testimonies, and tell us about their companions and their parents. This is a great experience in learning about them and about what their thought processes are and what their senses of values are.

I recall a missionary standing up and saying, "I have been in the mission field nine months, and I have had five companions." With a quivering chin and a choked-up voice, he said, "Never once in nine months have I had a companion who told me he loved me or appreciated what I was doing for him. I hope and pray that someday, somehow, I'll have a companion who will tell me that he loves me and appreciates me."

No matter where we come from, no matter what our family conditions are, we should learn and be appreciative of those circumstances which can build and lift us.

I recall another missionary who said, "Two weeks before I was to go see my bishop and tell him I was ready to go in the mission field, I had some doubts. I had some questions about the future and even about the Church. I walked into the living room and interrupted my father, who was watching television and said, 'Dad, I'm not so sure about Joseph Smith. I'm not so sure I know the Church is true. I'm not so sure I want to go out and represent it. I have a lot of questions and I have a lot of misgivings.' When I said that, my father walked over and turned off the television, took the cigarette he had in his hand and smashed it in the ashtray, took the can of beer he had in his other hand and put it down on the table, and said, 'Son, I want you to know that I don't do very much about it, but I know that the Church of Jesus Christ is true and that Joseph Smith is a prophet. I want you to hear me say it because I know that better than anything else in this world.'" This young man then said,

"I want my father to know that I appreciate him. He has some habits that he's not proud of. He has some habits that I'm not proud of. But he is my father and has a testimony, and I love him."

That kind of appreciation, that kind of maturity, will not only help a missionary to grow and develop, but will also be a great anchor in life's paths.

The most common question missionaries ask me is, "Elder Ashton, what can I do to get my mother or father or brother or sister more active in the Church? I realize now what they are missing and what they need. What can I do to get them active in the Church? What can I do to get them to become members of the Church?" In every case and every situation I have taken the opportunity to say, "The best way to get your family members active in the Church or to become members is to let them know that you appreciate them for what they do and what they stand for and tell them how much you love them." We need to express appreciation on a continuing basis, to love family members and neighbors into the Church.

The Savior has indicated in all that he has done the importance of gratitude and thanks and appreciation. Here are a few short quotations from the scriptures:

"He took the cup, and gave thanks." (Matthew 26:27.)

"He took the seven loaves and the fishes, and gave thanks." (Matthew 15:36.)

"Thou shalt thank the Lord thy God in all things." (D&C 59:7.)

"Ye must give thanks unto God in the Spirit for whatsoever blessing ye are blessed with." (D&C 46:32.)

"Let the peace of God rule in your hearts, . . . and be ye thankful." (Colossians 3:15.)

"Verily I say unto you my friends, fear not, let your hearts be comforted; yea, rejoice evermore, and in everything give thanks." (D&C 98:1.)

"When thou risest in the morning let thy heart be full of thanks unto God." (Alma 37:37.)

What a great day it will be in our lives when we can appreciate the blessing of appreciation and what it means to us!

Appreciation of companion, appreciation of sweetheart, appreciation of husband and wife is so important. It is a most important ingredient in a happy marriage. Many a family, many a marriage, is broken because of a lack of appreciation. The most mature and successful people who participate in marriage are those who understand appreciation. Is it any wonder that God has said we have two main things to do if we would avoid his wrath—to keep the commandments and to confess his hand in all things? (See D&C 59:21.) What a strength it is to have a companion who appreciates, feels, and expresses appreciation! How many times have you heard people say, "My marriage was terminated primarily because my husband (or wife) didn't appreciate anything I ever did for him. No matter what I did, there was no appreciation!"

God's love for us was so great that it was possible for him to endure and look upon the sufferings of his Only Begotten Son. We should be eternally grateful that God gave to us his Son, our Savior and Redeemer. Without him and his love and sacrifice, we could never be glorified in his eternal presence. The greatest gift of all, and the one for which we should be most appreciative, is the gift of his Son to us for purposes and realizations that we little comprehend today but should better understand with each passing hour.

How do we show appreciation for God's great gifts? How do we show appreciation for the gifts of parents, brothers and sisters, companions, friends, and associates? By our lives, by our works, and by our words, and through a willingness to confess his hand in this and in all other great gifts.

We are told that God is a jealous God—jealous lest we should ignore and fail to show appreciation for his greatest gift of all. "O give thanks unto the Lord; for he is good: for his mercy endureth for ever." (Psalm 106:1.)

Proper Self-Management

A successful football coach described his best player as an athlete who possesses an extra-special dimension. Besides being a great team man, he said, he performs well for himself. He possesses all the necessary physical and mental ingredients for success. He has personal pride and a good self-image. He has the bearing and self-conduct patterns that prompt his fellow team members and friends to say, "He's well balanced. He knows where he is going and how to get there."

Proper self-management is a great virtue that can lead to personal pride. Personal pride is a great motivator. It is a virtue to understand who we are and to conduct ourselves accordingly. To be created in God's image is a tremendous blessing with accompanying choice responsibilities.

"Know ye not that ye are the temple of God, and that the Spirit of God dwelleth in you? If any man defile the temple of God, him shall God destroy, for the temple of God is holy, which temple ye are." (1 Corinthians 3:16-17.)

Appropriate personal pride prohibits shabby performance. Proper self-image is a basic ingredient of pride in one's self. It is necessary if individual discipline is to be purposeful and effective.

Generally the cover or jacket of a book is designed to

sell what is inside. We will not have to die to be judged by the cover of the book of life. To those who would say, "It's what you really are inside that counts, not the length of the hair or beard," I would say, "If this is true, and I agree it is, why run the risk of looking like something you're not?" In regard to personal appearance, change can usually be brought about more quickly by courteously appealing to pride, impression, and image.

Self-image is often enhanced by the clothing worn. Appropriate, modest, flattering, and comfortable apparel helps a person feel good about himself. To be overdressed or immodestly dressed may create wrong impressions and improper identification. Improper clothing may also lead to wrong actions. I have always had a special amount of admiration and respect for blind friends who, even though they may be unable to see themselves or others, yet appear neat, well-dressed, and wellgroomed. The individual in that person's life is trying to help the blind person feel good about himself. We do ourselves and others a great injustice when we appear to be what we are not.

Reasonable questions to ask oneself could well be, "Am I proud of my appearance? Do my clothes properly introduce me?" What better example of proper personal appearance can we have than that glorious introduction shared with us by the Prophet Joseph Smith when he declared, "I saw two Personages, whose brightness and glory defy all description." (Joseph Smith—History 1:17.)

Taking the time to prepare oneself to look one's best for all occasions is grooming at its best. I am reminded of the mother who said, "It began to annoy me that the children would say, 'Where are you going, Mom?' whenever I took time out to tend to my hair, apply a little lipstick, or slip into a clean dress. Didn't I have the right to dress up at home? Then I started to realize how seldom I actually did dress up just to stay home and do housework. In fact, I rarely changed from my working clothes except when I went out to shop or visit. I had made myself too busy to bother with good grooming except for special occasions, for visiting, for going to church. No wonder the children got confused the rare times I made myself more presentable for no apparent reason at all."

One of life's eternal pursuits is learning to know oneself. Dr. Thomas Harris shares this worthy thought with us: "Most people never fulfill their human promise and potential because they remain perpetually helpless children overwhelmed by a sense of inferiority. The feeling of being okay does not imply that the person has risen above all his faults and emotional problems. It merely implies that he refuses to be paralyzed by them. He is determined to accept himself as he is but also to assume more and more control of his life."

Getting better acquainted with oneself and realizing God has given to every person gifts and talents is a worthy challenge. ". . . for there are many gifts, and to every man is given a gift by the Spirit of God. To some is given one, and to some is given another, that all may be profited thereby." (D&C 46:11-12.)

To be aware of one's limitations and potentials on a continuing basis will help in improved self-esteem. We need to be constantly aware of the fact that we are children of God. He knows us. He hears us. He loves us. Proper self-image will help us keep our habits, lives, and souls directed in happy paths. How proud we should be in the knowledge we have God-like attributes. It was Abraham Lincoln who said, "It is difficult to make a man miserable while he feels he is worthy of himself and claims kindred to the great God who made him."

Our obligation is to avoid self-pity, self-judgment, and self-indulgence. If we properly understand our relationship to God and his to us, we will not have moments, days, or lives spent in wondering, "What have I done to deserve this?" "What does God have against me?" or,

"Why wasn't I born with the talents my friends have?"

There needs to be a willingness and an ability on the part of all of us to properly relate to others in families, neighborhoods, and organizations. Courtesy and self-respect are necessary ingredients. We need the humble approach in dealing with others. Proper self-management will permit us to be a team member first, a coach, captain, or superstar second. In this relationship and way of life, the truth "If ye are not one ye are not mine" (D&C 38:27) takes on new significance.

Another important part of meaningful self-management is self-discipline, for the only discipline that really works is self-discipline. What can give greater satisfaction in life than mastery in self-conduct? Good health habits, integrity, bearing, mannerisms, conversation, and self-control can be powerful assets in one's personal balance sheet. These traits outwardly reflect the views of management. Integrity within oneself makes it possible for honesty with God, family, and all other associates. A person who has integrity within himself will also have it in his relationships with all others. A person walks uprightly only when he is moving in the right direction. He needs to know where he is going at all times and under all conditions. One avoids the appearance of evil as he follows paths that lead up and onward rather than down and out. Being anxiously engaged in worthy causes and seeking first the kingdom of God are external evidences of proper self-management and a proper application of personal resources.

To teach self-discipline, the emphasis should be on self-respect and esteem rather than the use of ridicule, embarrassment, and tears for conduct-improvement tools. One of the great tragedies that can come in a human's life is the destruction of self-respect. This destruction is often self-inflicted. Elevated expressions of human feelings, example, and courtesy build self-respect. People are lifted when they are treated as if they already were what they could be. It is my experience that most thinking people respond better to friendly persuasion than to threats or abuse.

Even personal health habits are generally improved by proper emphasis on temporal and eternal values rather than condemnation and disgust. Overweight people should be encouraged concerning appearance and health advantages of appropriate diet and trimness. Most will respond to honest appreciation expressed for what has been done or honestly attempted rather than caustic slurs.

Often self-discipline in personal health is weak or missing because we allow ourselves to become lost in revenge or spite attitudes. Recently I was talking to a young man on drugs. To the question, "Why do you use drugs?" he responded with, "To get even with my mom." From an attractive wife and young mother presently caught up in the habit of drinking cocktails: to my query, "Why are you involved in the use of alcohol?" she said, "That father-in-law of mine isn't going to tell me what to do!" If there are good reasons to be on drugs and alcohol, and at the present I don't know of any, there must be better reasons than those offered by these two friends. God and men glory in intelligent self-management.

As important to our self-image and general conduct as appropriate dress, grooming, and hair standards are moderation of voice, use of worthy language, good manners, respect for others' rights, and courtesy.

In any community or personal situation, it is refreshing and uplifting to see men and women who think, speak, and act with propriety. Good manners are necessary for the decency and peace of community living and should be a matter of grave concern to all, yet we hear and read less about their cultivation than we do about dieting and "daily dozens" to enhance our personal acceptance and development. Courtesy is at its best when it is least obvious. Courtesy is not the invention of a past generation; rather, it is but a long-standing manner of life. We need to be reminded of the fact that Moses did more than bring down the Ten Commandments from the mount; in unmistakable terms he prescribed the conduct of a gentleman—civility to friends and strangers, respect for the blind, the deaf, the aged, the weary, and the unsuspecting, and abstention from tale-bearing.

Courtesy is not unusual conduct to be reserved for a special circle of friends or circumstances. It is not a veneer to be put on for special social occasions or people. It is a way of life of tremendous significance, whether it be in the home, in the office, or on the highway. It cushions the unexpected and eases our jolts wonderfully. We cannot justify or condone discourtesy regardless of friendship or situation. Our best manners learned and used in the home will appropriately surface in our associations with all persons.

Being on time to appointments and meetings is a phase of self-discipline and an evidence of self-respect. Punctuality is a courteous compliment the intelligent person pays to his associates. Punctuality or the lack thereof oftentimes is the only introduction one will ever have to new groups and friends. Serenity and poise are not the companions of those who lack the courtesy and judgment to be on time.

He is well disciplined who develops patience in his dealings with his fellowmen. In conversation he is considerate and knows how to listen. A courteous conversationalist is not a boaster, a babbler, or a boor. Wise is the man who says what needs to be said, but not all that could be said.

May we look to ourselves with new responsibility, new self-appreciation, higher self-image, and greater self-respect. We are children of God. We do possess God-given attributes. We do have the opportunity and obligation to learn to be leaders. Let us so live that it may be said of us, "He is well balanced. He knows where he is going and how to get there. He is a good manager of himself." By doing this it will be possible for us to better serve in the kingdom and have a greater appreciation for the thrilling declaration, "As man now is, God once was. As God now is, man may become." (Lorenzo Snow.) This is what proper self-management is all about.

Managing Your Money

Recently I had the opportunity to visit with a choice young couple. They were to be married within the week. Their eyes sparkled in anticipation of the important event and their continuing love for one another. Both had the advantages of college education, good homes, and cultural experiences. It was delightful to share their personalities, plans, and potentials. Their courtship already seemed appropriately launched on an eternal basis.

During our interview, their responses to only one question gave me concern. I hope my anxieties and suggestions caused them to reassess their pending partnership future.

To the question, "Who is going to manage the money in your marriage?" she said, "He is, I guess," while he responded, "We haven't talked about that yet." These comments surprised and shocked me.

How important are money management and finances in marriage and family affairs? May I respond, "Tremendously." The American Bar Association recently indicated that 89 percent of all divorces could be traced to quarrels and accusations over money. Others have estimated that 75 percent of all divorces result from clashes over finances. Some professional counselors indicated that four out of five families are strapped with serious money problems.

May I at this time hasten to emphasize the fact that these marriage tragedies are not caused simply by lack of money, but rather by the mismanagement of personal finances. A prospective wife could well concern herself not with the amount her husband-to-be can earn in a month, but rather how will he manage the money that comes into his hands. Money management should take precedence over money productivity. A prospective husband who is engaged to a sweetheart who has everything would do well to take yet another look and see if she has money management sense.

In the home, money management between husband and wife should be on a partnership basis, with both parties having a voice in decision and policy making. When children come along and reach the age of accountability, they too should be involved in money concerns on a limited partnership basis. Peace, contentment, love, and security in the home are not possible when financial anxieties and bickerings prevail. Whether we are anticipating marriage or are well into it, today is the time for all of us to review and repent as necessary to improve our money management skills and live within our means.

May I make some recommendations for improved personal and family financial management, since proper money management and living within one's means are essential in today's world if we are to live abundantly and happily. The following twelve points will help each of us achieve this goal, I believe.

1. *Teach family members early the importance of working and earning.* "In the sweat of thy face shalt thou eat bread" is not outdated counsel. It is basic to personal welfare.

One of the greatest favors parents can do for their children is to teach them to work. Much has been said over the years about children and monthly allowances, and opinions and recommendations vary greatly. I'm from the "old school." I believe that children should earn their money needs through service and appropriate chores. I think it is unfortunate for a child to grow up in a home where the seed is planted in the child's mind that there is a family money tree that automatically drops "green stuff" once a week or once a month.

2. *Teach children to make money decisions in keeping with their capacities to comprehend.* "Save your money" is a hollow pronouncement from a parent to a child. "Save your money for a mission, bicycle, doll house, trousseau, or car" makes understandable sense.

Family unity comes from saving together for a common, jointly approved purpose. In our home we found it unifying to have a child save for a major project and then, when the amount was achieved, we matched it with a predetermined percentage, similar to what the Church does with the wards and stakes in building and real estate matters.

3. *Teach each family member to contribute to the total family welfare.* Encourage fun projects, understandable to the children, that contribute to a family goal of joy. Some families miss a tremendous financial and spiritual experience when they fail to sit together, preferably during family home evening, and each put in his share of the monthly amount going to the son or daughter, brother or sister who is serving in the mission field. When this monthly activity is engaged in all at once, he or she becomes "our" missionary with pride becoming a two-way street.

4. *Teaching family members to pay financial obligations promptly is part of integrity and honesty development.* Paying tithing promptly to Him who does not come to check up each month will teach us to be more honest with those physically closer at hand.

5. *Learn to manage money before it manages you.* A bride-

to-be would do well to ask herself, "Can my sweetheart manage money? Does he know how to live within his means?" These are more important questions than "Can he earn a lot of money?" New attitudes and relationships toward money should be developed constantly by all couples. After all, the partnership should be full and eternal.

6. *Learn self-discipline and self-restraint in money matters.* Such conduct can be more important than courses in accounting. Married couples show genuine maturity when they think of their partners and their families ahead of their own spending impulses.

Money management skills should be learned together in a spirit of cooperation and love on a continuing basis. A disgusted husband once said, "I know that in life money talks, but when my wife gets hold of it, all it ever says is 'goodbye.' " To the husband who says his wife is the poorest money manager in the world, I would say, "Look in the mirror and meet the world's poorest teacher-trainer."

7. *Use a budget.* Avoid finance charges except for homes, education, and other vital investments. Buy consumer durables with cash. Avoid installment credit and be careful with your use of credit cards. They are principally for convenience and should not be used carelessly or recklessly. Buy used items until you have saved sufficient to purchase quality new items. Save and invest a specific percent of your income. Learn the principle of obedience as you make your Church contributions, and meet your financial obligations promptly.

Please listen carefully to this—and if it makes some of you feel uncomfortable, it is on purpose: Latter-day Saints who ignore or avoid their creditors are entitled to feel the inner frustrations that such conduct merits, and they are not living as Latter-day Saints should!

8. *Make education a continuing process.* Complete as much formal, full-time education as possible. This in-

cludes the trade schools. This is money well invested. Use night school and correspondence classes to further prepare. Acquire some special skill or ability that could be used to avoid prolonged unemployment. In these days of worldwide heavy unemployment, we should not allow ourselves, when we are out of work, to sit back and wait for "our type of job" if other honorable interim employment becomes available.

9. *Work toward home ownership.* This qualifies as an investment, not consumption. Buy the type of home your income will support. Improve the home and beautify the landscape all the time you occupy the premises so that if you do sell it, you can use the capital gain to get a better home.

10. *Appropriately involve yourself in an insurance program.* It is most important to have sufficient medical and adequate life insurance.

11. *Strive to understand and cope with existing inflation.* Learn to see through the money illusion and recognize the real value of money. Most wage earners today have less purchasing power than they did in 1973. To some degree inflation is probably going to be with us for a long time. Realize that you are living in a new era of higher prices and less abundant energy.

12. *Appropriately involve yourself in a food storage program.* Accumulate your basic supplies in a systematic and an orderly way. Avoid going into debt for these purposes. Beware of unwise promotional schemes.

These few points and suggestions are not intended to be all-inclusive or exhaustive. Rather, it is hoped that a need has been brought to the surface for our serious consideration. We need to recognize and be aware of these basic guidelines for wise money management.

God help us to realize that money management is an important ingredient in proper personal welfare. Learning to live within our means should be a continuing process. We need to work constantly toward keeping ourselves free of financial difficulties. It is a happy day financially when time and interest are working for you and not against you.

Money in the lives of Latter-day Saints should be used as a means of achieving eternal happiness. Careless and selfish uses cause us to live in financial bondage. We can't afford to neglect personal and family involvement in our money management. God will open the windows of heaven to us in these matters if we will but live close to him and keep his commandments.

He Took Him By the Hand

"Jesus took him by the hand, and lifted him up; and he arose." (Mark 9:27.) The day is here when if we are to follow in Jesus' paths, we must take the weary, lonely, depressed, the troubled soul and the gospel-hungry by the hand and lift and help. Yes, we also need to lift the dishonest, the self-condemning, and those who have chosen expediency over correct principles. Countless numbers may be able to take their first steps in the right direction when we are willing to provide a lift of confidence and encouragement and give them back self-respect.

The Savior taught these truths to his disciples in his story of the last judgment, when the King will say, "For I was an hungred, and ye gave me meat: I was thirsty, and ye gave me drink: I was a stranger, and ye took me in: Naked, and ye clothed me: I was sick, and ye visited me: I was in prison, and ye came unto me." (Matthew 25:35-36.)

Perhaps we can appropriately add, "I was down, and ye lifted me up. My soul was sick, and ye comforted me. My steps were unsteady, and ye took my hand. I was uncertain, and ye lifted me to paths of security."

How beautiful in the eyes of the Lord are those who are spiritually well, those who have been taken by the hand and lifted up and made spiritually whole. How beautiful in the eyes of the Lord are those who take the time to lift the needy hand. Peace of mind comes to us only when we are spiritually healed. True joy comes from within. Freedom from a troubled soul is a worthy goal. Many were healed physically from ailments and suffering during the Savior's ministry, but real joy and happiness were not always realized. People may be healed but not lifted. Happiness does not come from physical, social, or economic success. "A man's life consisteth not in the abundance of things which he possesseth." (Luke 12:15.)

Frequently the Savior admonished the physically healed to boast not of their new strength, but rather to go their way, walking in truth and using their new powers to lift others. There is evidence that many were healed physically but remained undisciplined and spiritually ill. "Return unto me, and repent of your sins, and be converted, that I may heal you," the Savior said. (3 Nephi 9:13.)

Healings are not to be made the subject of pride and boasting. Rather, healings should be used to lift self and others to greater heights and service. May we not appropriately conclude that the lift can be more important than the healing.

Certainly the greatest miracles of our day are the lifting and healing of troubled souls. Spiritual strength is a priceless possession available to those who will endure in righteousness. The healing of the troubled soul gives health and strength to those dead in things righteous. Purity, faith, hope, and charity are restored, making whole those who were once spiritually sick. This healing comes through conversion to truth and adherence to correct principles. We have the scriptural promise that Christ "shall rise from the dead, with healing in his wings; and all those who shall believe on his name shall be saved in the kingdom of God." (2 Nephi 25:13.) Spiritual death and spiritual sickness vanish for those who would be healed by Christ and his atoning sacrifice.

President Harold B. Lee once said, in speaking to the priesthood, "In your hands is given a sacred trust not only to have the authority to act in the name of the Lord, but to so prepare yourselves as clean and pure vessels that the power of Almighty God may be manifested through you as you officiate in the sacred ordinances of the priesthood." Yes, in our hands is not only the power and authority to act, but also the strength to lift if we remain true and faithful.

In this great church we must try to lift those who need us economically, socially, physically, and spiritually as we earnestly link hands with the Lord. He has told us: "This is my work and my glory—to bring to pass the immortality and eternal life of man." (Moses 1:39.)

A beautiful lesson is taught in the experience of Peter and John, who went up together into the temple to pray:

"And a certain man lame from his mother's womb was carried, whom they laid daily at the gate of the temple which is called Beautiful, to ask alms of them that entered into the temple:

"Who seeing Peter and John about to go into the temple asked an alms.

"And Peter, fastening his eyes upon him with John, said, Look on us.

"And he gave heed unto them, expecting to receive something of them.

"Then Peter said, Silver and gold have I none; but such as I have give I thee: In the name of Jesus Christ of Nazareth rise up and walk.

"And he took him by the right hand, and lifted him up: and immediately his feet and ancle bones received strength.

"And he leaping up stood, and walked, and entered with them into the temple, walking, and leaping, and praising God.

"And all the people saw him walking and praising God." (Acts 3:1-9.)

This man did not know he could walk until Peter took him by the hand and lifted him. He didn't realize or believe he could now walk and go forth on his own until this initial lift started him on his way. Peter was able to lift him because he stood on high ground in God's service.

In this area of thinking, lifting, and taking by the hand, it seems to me that a scripture that is often misunderstood is this: "Therefore shall a man leave his father and mother, and shall cleave unto his wife: and they shall be one flesh." (Genesis 2:24.) Certainly a married man should cleave unto his wife in faithfulness, protection, comfort, and total support, but in leaving father, mother, and other family members, it was never intended that they now be ignored, abandoned, shunned, or deserted. They are still a family, a great source of strength, a refuge, a delight, and an eternal unit. Wise parents whose children have left to start their own families realize that their family role still continues, not in a realm of domination, control, regulation, supervision, or imposition, but in love, concern, and encouragement. Many a full-time missionary has been heard to say, "I received some of my best letters while away, from a grandmother, an aunt, or a brother-in-law." Others have said, "My father passed away some years ago, but my uncle or grandfather is keeping me financially in the mission field." The whole family belongs to us and we to them. What a blessing! What a sacred obligation!

The Prophet Joseph Smith valued this continuing source of strength. On many occasions he fervently prayed for the improved health of his ailing father so that he might "be blessed with his company and advice, esteeming it one of the greatest earthly blessings to be blessed with the society of parents, whose mature years and experience render them capable of administering the most wholesome advice." (*History of the Church* 2:289.) Can we not appropriately remind ourselves that though he were a prophet, yet learned he from the wisdom and love of a good family?

Joseph once said of his brother Hyrum: "There was Brother Hyrum who took me by the hand—a natural brother. Thought I to myself, Brother Hyrum, what a faithful heart you have got! O may the Eternal Jehovah crown eternal blessings upon your head, as a reward for the care you have had for my soul!" (*HC* 5:107-8.) "I could pray in my heart that all my brethren were like unto my beloved brother Hyrum, who possesses the mildness of a lamb, and the integrity of a Job, and in short, the meekness and humility of Christ; and I love him with that love that is stronger than death, for I never had occasion to rebuke him, nor he me." (*HC* 2:338.)

Often the greatest lifts we receive come from within the ranks of our families. Sometimes the hands needed most are those closest to us. Often the hands closest to us are the strongest. When we begin to realize this relationship, one family member to another, we begin to understand the basics of our great welfare services programs, which are the gospel of Jesus Christ in action. God has decreed that family members are to help family members. God has decreed that family members are to be a blessing to family members. When some of us in a discouraged frame of mind identify a family member as not worth a hand or a lift, may I remind us that when we continue to lift, regardless of the apparent results, added strength is ours. The more we lift, the more we are able to lift.

Worthy Latter-day Saint marriages are forever; and as we cleave to the one most precious to us, we are entitled to the blessings of the total family. The family lift will be available to us. We must take family members by the hand and show them that our love is real and continuing. When we take someone by the hand, both hands are left stronger. No one ever lifted someone else without stepping toward higher ground. We must make our home ties strong and available to all family members. Our homes should be places to which our children will want to come.

If we keep the commandments of God and walk hand in hand with him in his paths, Satan cannot touch us. Faithful members of the Church do not have to walk alone. The troubled soul need not find its way back alone. God's hand is available to all if we will but reach out and up.

"Jesus took him [one possessed of a foul spirit] by the hand, and lifted him up; and he arose.

"And when he [Jesus] was come into the house, his disciples asked him privately, Why could not we cast him out?

"And he said unto them, This kind can come forth by nothing, but by prayer and fasting." (Mark 9:27-29.)

I pray our Heavenly Father to help us so live that we may have that inner strength and power to take those about us by the hand and lift.

The Magic of the Name

One of the many evidences I have of Joseph Smith's being a true prophet of God is his account of the conversation he had in answer to his humble in-the-grove prayer.

"But, exerting all my powers to call upon God to deliver me out of the power of this enemy which had seized upon me, and at the very moment when I was ready to sink into despair and abandon myself to destruction—not to an imaginary ruin, but to the power of some actual being from the unseen world, who had such marvelous power as I had never before felt in any being—just at this moment of great alarm, I saw a pillar of light exactly over my head, above the brightness of the sun, which descended gradually until it fell upon me.

"It no sooner appeared than I found myself delivered from the enemy which held me bound. When the light rested upon me I saw two Personages, whose brightness and glory defy all description, standing above me in the air. One of them spake unto me, calling me by name and said, pointing to the other—*This is My Beloved Son. Hear Him!*" (Joseph Smith—History 1:16-17.)

When skeptics, doubters, ridiculers, and enemies harassed this fourteen-year-old boy with, "If you've seen God and his Son, Jesus Christ, as you claim, tell us what they said to you," with conviction he declared, "One of them called me 'Joseph.' " Just think of the rapture that filled his bosom when he saw the living God. God knew and called him by name!

On September 21, 1823, Joseph Smith reported a visit from a heavenly messenger. There appeared in his room an angel who called him by name and gave him instructions. Joseph wrote:

". . . after I had retired to my bed for the night, I betook myself to prayer and supplication to Almighty God for forgiveness of all my sins and follies, and also for a manifestation to me, that I might know of my state and standing before him; for I had full confidence in obtaining a divine manifestation, as I previously had one.

"While I was thus in the act of calling upon God, I discovered a light appearing in my room, which continued to increase until the room was lighter than at noonday, when immediately a personage appeared at my bedside, standing in the air, for his feet did not touch the floor.

"He had on a loose robe of most exquisite whiteness. It was a whiteness beyond anything earthly I had ever seen; nor do I believe that any earthly thing could be made to appear so exceedingly white and brilliant. His hands were naked, and his arms also, a little above the wrist; so, also, were his feet naked, as were his legs, a little above the ankles. His head and neck were also bare. I could discover that he had no other clothing on but this robe, as it was open, so that I could see into his bosom.

"Not only was his robe exceedingly white, but his whole person was glorious beyond description, and his countenance truly like lightning. The room was exceedingly light, but not so very bright as immediately around his person. When I first looked upon him, I was afraid; but the fear soon left me.

"*He called me by name,* and said unto me that he was a messenger sent from the presence of God to me, and that his *name was Moroni;* that God had a work for me to do;

and that *my name* should be had for good and evil among all nations, kindreds, and tongues, or that it should be both good and evil spoken of among all people."

The angel appeared in Joseph's room two more times that night and repeated the same message. The next morning Joseph was working in the fields with his father when he became so weak and felt so fatigued that his father told him to go home. While attempting to cross a fence, he found his strength totally leaving him, and he fell helpless and unconscious on the ground.

"The first thing that I can recollect was a voice speaking unto me, *calling me by name.* I looked up, and beheld the same messenger standing over my head, surrounded by light as before. He then again related unto me all that he had related to me the previous night, and commanded me to go to my father and tell him of the vision and commandments which I had received." (Joseph Smith—History 1:29-33, 49. Italics added.)

It is significant that Moroni called Joseph by name in each incident.

In Matthew we read how Joseph was deeply concerned because Mary, to whom he was espoused, "was found with child of the Holy Ghost. . . . But while he thought on these things, behold, the angel of the Lord appeared unto him in a dream, saying, Joseph, thou son of David, fear not to take unto thee Mary thy wife: for that which is conceived in her is of the Holy Ghost. And she shall bring forth a son, and thou shalt call his name Jesus. . . ." (Matthew 1:18, 20-21.)

Again, an angel of the Lord called Joseph by name, and also revealed to him the name of the child who was to be born. How important are names in singling out each individual! Let me refer to one more example from the Bible, that of Mary Magdalene at the sepulchre, as we ponder the magic of the name.

"Jesus saith unto her, Woman, why weepest thou? whom seekest thou? She, supposing him to be the

127

gardener, saith unto him, Sir, if thou have borne him hence, tell me where thou hast laid him, and I will take him away.

"Jesus saith unto her, *Mary*. She turned herself, and saith unto him, Rabboni; which is to say, Master.

"Jesus saith unto her, Touch me not; for I am not yet ascended to my *Father;* but go to my brethren, and say unto them, I ascend unto my *Father,* and your *Father;* and to my *God,* and your *God.*

"*Mary Magdalene* came and told the disciples that she had seen the Lord, and that he had spoken these things unto her." (John 20:15-18. Italics added.)

Following the death and funeral of President Joseph Fielding Smith, the Council of the Twelve went to the upper room in the Salt Lake Temple to organize the First Presidency. Through inspiration and revelation the will of the Lord had borne witness to all that Harold B. Lee was to be ordained and set apart. The first words Elder Lee said were, "Spencer, will you be voice?" The first thing President Spencer W. Kimball said in performing the ordinance and setting apart, surrounded by his associates of the Twelve, was, "Harold Bingham Lee."

My first contact with President Lee was shortly after I was married. A number of us, including President Lee and his wife, were at the summer home of Adelle Howells, the general president of the Primary; we gathered for a home Sunday School. Though I had never met President Lee before, he walked over to me and said, "Marv, will you conduct the Sunday School?" I was thrilled and shocked. He knew my name and called me by name. I felt at that time, "He is my friend. He knows me." Not only would I conduct that meeting, but I was ready to do anything for him. President Lee was always a master in calling people by name; he warmed hearts and won friends by calling them by name.

I recall well an experience I had with my mission president, Hugh B. Brown. We missionaries were playing in a championship British National Basketball tournament game in London, England, in 1938. It was the last quarter of the game and our team was trailing by a few points. As I ran down the floor with my teammates in a determined effort to achieve victory, I recall hearing President Brown from the sidelines shout, "Marv, we want this game!" In the excitement he called me "Marv" instead of "Elder Ashton." I knew he was serious. The Church needed the favorable publicity accompanying the victory. I passed the word to my associates that President Brown was serious in his desire for our victory. Happily we went on to win. He called me by name, and we responded with the needed extra push.

What are the first two words in the Book of Mormon? "*I, Nephi.*" What are the first words in the Lord's prayer? "*Our Father* which art in heaven, *Hallowed be thy name.*" (Matthew 6:9. Italics added.)

Recall with me the heavenly voice that said, "Saul, Saul, why persecuteth thou me?" (Acts 9:4.)

Brigham Young's dying words were, "Joseph, Joseph, Joseph." Joseph Smith's dying words in the Carthage Jail were "Oh Lord, my God."

When we ordain and set apart, the name comes first, as in administering to the sick. In administering the sacrament the first words are "Oh God, the Eternal Father."

All our prayers are given and asked in the name of Jesus Christ. "And thou shalt continue in calling upon God in my name." (D&C 24:5.) "Wherefore, let all men beware how *they take my name* in their lips—For behold, verily I say, that many there be who are under this condemnation, who use the name of the Lord, and use it in vain, having not authority." (D&C 63:61-62. Italics added.)

"Yea, even twelve; and the Twelve shall be my disciples, and they shall *take upon them my name;* and the Twelve are they who shall desire *to take upon them my name* with full purpose of heart. And if they desire *to take upon them my name* with full purpose of heart, they are called to go into all the world to preach my gospel unto every creature." (D&C 18:27-28. Italics added.)

"The person who is called of God and has authority from Jesus Christ to baptize, shall go down into the water with the person who has presented himself or herself for baptism, and shall say, *calling him or her by name:* Having been commissioned of Jesus Christ, I baptize you *in the name* of the Father, and of the Son, and of the Holy Ghost. Amen." (D&C 20:73. Italics added.)

Members of the Council of the Twelve are special witnesses in the name of Christ in all of the world of his divinity and reality. He is our Master, our Savior, our Redeemer.

I recall a surprise visit to a ward MIA meeting many years ago. Upon introducing myself, I was invited to sit on the stand. A frustrated presiding officer, when it was time for the opening prayer, stood and looked at a young Scout-age boy and said, "You on the second row, third one over, come up and say the prayer." I was disappointed. She had failed to call him by name. Later I suggested to her the importance of calling people by name in our roles as leaders and parents.

I recall walking through the corridor at the Utah State Prison with the warden some time ago on the way to the chapel. As we walked down the long hall I noticed three or four inmates gathered in one of the corners. I asked the warden, "What's the big fellow's name?" "Gayle Boone," he said. The warden was then called away and I was left alone to go to the chapel. As I approached the men, I said to the heavily muscled one, "Hi, Gayle." Gayle left his young friend and trailed me down to the chapel. "How did you know my name?" he asked hesitatingly. He followed me and liked me because I had taken the time to learn and use his name.

The magic of the name is often a key to leadership. Most people respond to the magic of their names and are lifted when they are mentioned. We all like to do business, including our Father's business, with people who know us and call us by name. Let us ever be aware that God set the pattern for us when he called Joseph by name. We too will be more effective in our relationships if we appropriately use the name of each person with whom we associate.

"Nobody Is a Nobody"

One winter when the Salt Lake area was experiencing one of its worst snowstorms, a handsome young serviceman and his beautiful bride-to-be encountered extreme difficulty in getting to the Salt Lake Temple for their marriage appointment. She was in one location in the valley and he was to come from another nearby town. Heavy snows and winds had closed the highways during the night and early morning hours. After many hours of anxious waiting, some of us were able to help them get to the temple and be married before the day was over. How grateful they, their families, and friends were for assistance and concern in their keeping this most important appointment. The young bridegroom expressed his deep gratitude with, "Thank you very much for all you did to make our wedding possible. I don't understand why you went to all this trouble to help me. Really, I'm nobody." I am sure he meant his comment to be a most sincere compliment, but I responded to it firmly, but I hope kindly, with, "Bill, I have never helped a 'nobody' in my life. In the kingdom of our Heavenly Father nobody is a 'nobody.' "

This tendency to wrongfully identify ourselves was again brought to my attention during an interview with a troubled wife. Her marriage was in great difficulty. She had tried earnestly to correct the communication blocks with her husband but with little success. She was grateful for the time her bishop spent in counseling. Her stake president was also most patient and understanding in his willingness to try to help. Her many contacts with properly channeled priesthood direction left her not only grateful, but somewhat amazed. Her concluding observation was, "I just don't understand all of you people giving so much time and showing so much concern. After all, I'm really nobody."

I am certain our Heavenly Father is displeased when we refer to ourselves as "nobody." How fair are we when we classify ourselves a "nobody"? How fair are we to our families? How fair are we to God? We do ourselves a great injustice when we allow ourselves, through tragedy, misfortune, challenge, discouragement, or whatever the earthly situation, to so identify ourselves. No matter how or where we find ourselves, we cannot with any justification label ourselves "nobody." As children of God we are somebody. He will build us, mold us, and magnify us if we will but hold our heads up, our arms out, and walk with him. What a great blessing to be created in his image and know of our true potential in and through him! What a great blessing to know that in his strength we can do all things!

Ammon taught a great lesson not only to his brother Aaron, but also to all of us in this day:

"And it came to pass that when Ammon said these words, his brother Aaron rebuked him, saying: Ammon, I fear that joy doth carry thee away unto boasting.

"But Ammon said unto him: I do not boast in my own strength, nor in my own wisdom; but behold, my joy is full, yea, my heart is brim with joy, and I will rejoice in my God.

"Yea, I know that . . . as to my strength I am weak; therefore I will not boast of myself, but I will boast of my God, for in his strength I can do all things; yea, behold, many mighty miracles we have wrought in this land, for which we will praise his name forever." (Alma 26:10-12.)

As grievous as labeling ourselves "nobody" is our tendency to classify another as a "nobody." Sometimes people are prone to identify the stranger or the unknown as a nobody. Often this is done for self-convenience and an unwillingness to listen. Countless numbers today reject Joseph Smith and his message because they will not accept a fourteen-year-old "nobody." Others turn away from eternal restored truths available today because they will not accept a nineteen-year-old elder or a twenty-one-year-old lady missionary or a neighbor down the street because they are "nobody," so they may suppose. There is no doubt in my mind that one of the reasons our Savior Jesus Christ was rejected and crucified was because in the eyes of the world he was blindly viewed as a "nobody," humbly born in a manger, an advocate of such strange doctrine as "Peace on earth, good will toward men."

I bear witness that Joseph Smith knew with earth-shattering impact he was somebody when in answer to humble prayer, God appeared with his Son, Jesus Christ, and spoke unto him, calling him by name. Through the centuries God has often chosen what the world would classify as a "nobody" to bear his truths. Listen to Joseph Smith's thoughts and self-analysis in this area:

"It caused me serious reflection then, and often has since, how very strange it was that an obscure boy, of a little over fourteen years of age, and one, too, who was doomed to the necessity of obtaining a scanty maintenance by his daily labor, should be thought a character of sufficient importance to attract the attention of the great ones of the most popular sects of the day, and in a manner to create in them a spirit of the most bitter persecution and reviling. But strange or not, so it was, and it was the cause of great sorrow to myself. However, it was nevertheless a fact that I had beheld a vision." (Joseph Smith—History 1:23-24.)

135

May I remind all of us Joseph Smith referred to himself as "an obscure boy" but never as a "nobody." He was sustained all the days of his perilous life by the knowledge that in God's strength he could accomplish all things.

God help us to realize that one of our greatest responsibilities and privileges is to lift a self-labeled "nobody" to a "somebody" who is wanted, needed, and desirable. Our first obligation in this area of stewardship is to begin with self. "I am nobody" is a destructive philosophy. It is a tool of the deceiver. It is heartbreaking when youth in difficulty look up and respond to offered guidance with, "What does it matter? I'm nobody." It is just as disturbing when a student on campus responds with, "I am no one special on campus. I'm just one of the thousands. I'm really nobody."

May we learn an important lesson from a missionary I once interviewed. In answer to the question, "How often do you receive letters from your parents," the elder replied, "Very, very seldom." "What are you doing about it?" I asked. "I'm still writing them every week," he declared. Here was a young man who may have had some excuse to pity himself with a "nobody" label when his parents didn't bother to write, but he was having no part of this kind of attitude. Further conversation with him emphatically convinced me that here was a young man who is really someone. If his parents didn't write, that was their responsibility. His responsibility was to write, and that is just what he was doing with enthusiasm. I have never met this missionary's mother or father, probably never will, but wherever they are, in my mind they are "somebody" just to have him for their son. This missionary will succeed because he knows he is someone, and is conducting himself accordingly.

To mothers, fathers, husbands, wives, and children everywhere, I declare that regardless of your present station in life, you are someone special. Remember, you may be an obscure boy, girl, man, or woman, but you are not a "nobody." Please enjoy with me one of the truly great parables in all of the Holy Scriptures as we think along this subject.

"A certain man had two sons:

"And the younger of them said to his father, Father, give me the portion of goods that falleth to me. And he divided unto them his living.

"And not many days after the younger son gathered all together, and took his journey into a far country, and there wasted his substance with riotous living.

"And when he had spent all, there arose a mighty famine in that land; and he began to be in want.

"And he went and joined himself to a citizen of that country; and he sent him into his fields to feed swine.

"And he would fain have filled his belly with the husks that the swine did eat: and no man gave unto him.

"And when he came to himself, he said, How many hired servants of my father's have bread enough and to spare, and I perish with hunger!

"I will arise and go to my father, and will say unto him, Father, I have sinned against heaven, and before thee,

"And am no more worthy to be called thy son: make me as one of thy hired servants.

"And he arose, and came to his father. But when he was yet a great way off, his father saw him, and had compassion, and ran, and fell on his neck, and kissed him.

"And the son said unto him, Father, I have sinned against heaven, and in thy sight, and am no more worthy to be called thy son.

"But the father said to his servants, Bring forth the best robe, and put it on him; and put a ring on his hand, and shoes on his feet:

"And bring hither the fatted calf, and kill it; and let us eat, and be merry:

"For this my son was dead, and is alive again; he was lost, and is found. And they began to be merry.

"Now his elder son was in the field: and as he came and drew nigh to the house, he heard musick and dancing.

"And he called one of the servants, and asked what these things meant.

"And he said unto him, Thy brother is come; and thy father hath killed the fatted calf, because he hath received him safe and sound.

"And he was angry, and would not go in: therefore came his father out, and intreated him.

"And he answering said to his father, Lo, these many years do I serve thee, neither transgressed I at any time thy commandment; and yet thou never gavest me a kid, that I might make merry with my friends:

"But as soon as this thy son was come, which hath devoured thy living with harlots, thou hast killed for him the fatted calf.

"And he said unto him, Son, thou art ever with me, and all that I have is thine.

"It was meet that we should make merry, and be glad; for this thy brother was dead, and is alive again; and was lost, and is found." (Luke 15:11-32.)

Think well again on these points, if you will. "Father, divide your goods and give me my share. I am going off on my own." In the days ahead the young man wasted his possessions with riotous living. He became so low and so hungry that he lived with the swine. His heart was crying out, "I am lower than the low. I am now absolutely nothing—I am absolutely nobody." Please weigh the impact of the father's response. He saw the son coming, and he ran to him and kissed him, and placed his best robe on him. Then he killed the fatted calf, and they made merry together. This self-declared "nobody" was his son; "he was dead and is alive again; he was lost and is found again."

In the father's joy he also taught well his older, bewildered son that he, too, was someone. "Son, thou art ever with me, and *all* that I have is thine." Contemplate, if you will, the depth—yes, even the eternal proportions—of the words, "all that I have is thine." I declare with all the strength I possess we have a Heavenly Father who claims and loves all of us regardless of where our steps have taken us. We are his sons and his daughters, and he loves us.

We must never allow ourselves to be self-condemning. We must avoid discouragement, and teach ourselves correct principles and govern ourselves with honor. As we develop proper self-image in ourselves and others, the "nobody" attitude will completely disappear.

God lives. He, too, is someone—real and eternal—and he wants us to be someone with him. I bear witness that in his strength we can become like him.

What Is a Friend?

Someone has said, "A friend is a person who is willing to take me the way I am." Accepting this as one definition of the word, may I quickly suggest that we are something less than a real friend if we leave a person the same way we find him.

There seems to be a misunderstanding on the part of some persons today as to what it means to be a friend. Acts of a friend should result in self-improvement, better attitudes, self-reliance, comfort, consolation, self-respect, and better welfare. Certainly the word *friend* is misused if it is identified with a person who contributes to our delinquency, misery, and heartaches. When we make a man feel he is wanted, his whole attitude changes. Our friendship will be recognizable if our actions and attitudes result in improvement and independence.

It takes courage to be a real friend. Some of us endanger the valued classification of friend because of our unwillingness to be one under all circumstances. Fear can deprive us of friendship. Some of us identify our closest friends as those with the courage to remain and share themselves with us under all circumstances. A friend is a person who will suggest and render the best for us regardless of the immediate consequences. Winston Churchill became Great Britain's greatest friend in his country's darkest hour because he was courageous enough to call for "blood, toil, tears and sweat" when some would have accepted him more readily as a friend had he advocated peaceful surrender.

President Abraham Lincoln was once criticized for his attitude toward his enemies. "Why do you try to make friends of them?" asked an associate. "You should try to destroy them." "Am I not destroying my enemies," Lincoln gently replied, "when I make them my friends?"

Are we not within our rights as members of The Church of Jesus Christ of Latter-day Saints to regard our Prophet, Seer, and Revelator as a close, personal friend as he leaves us improved daily by his willingness to reprove, admonish, love, encourage, and guide according to our needs?

As we strive to comprehend more fully the significance of friendship, the more our appreciation should increase for the truths found in the writings of James: "Pure religion and undefiled before God and the Father is this, To visit the fatherless and widows in their affliction, and to keep himself unspotted from the world." (James 1:27.) It is well for us to be reminded we are friends to ourselves when we keep our lives unspotted from the sins of the world and leave ourselves better tomorrow than we are today. It is a worthy goal to be a true friend to oneself. Our responsibility to the widow and the fatherless is to accept them as we find them, but not to leave them without improvement. Ours is to lift the heavy heart, say the encouraging word, and assist in supplying the daily needs. Aren't we something less than a friend if we have the gospel of Jesus Christ and are unwilling to share it by word and example with a family, a member, a neighbor, or a stranger?

A friend is a possession we earn, not a gift. "Ye are my friends, if ye do whatsoever I command you." (John 15:14.) The Lord has declared that those who serve him and keep his commandments are called his servants. After they have been tested and tried and are found faithful and true in all things, they are no longer called servants, but friends. His friends are the ones whom he will take into his kingdom and with whom he will associate in an eternal inheritance. (D&C 93:45-46.)

Let me share with you quickly a few of the many "friend" references in the Doctrine and Covenants referred to by our Savior.

"And again, verily I say unto you, my friends, . . . Draw near unto me and I will draw near unto you; seek me diligently and ye shall find me; ask, and ye shall receive; knock, and it shall be opened unto you. Whatsoever ye ask the Father in my name it shall be given unto you, that is expedient for you." (D&C 88:62-64.)

". . . my friends Sidney and Joseph." (D&C 100:1.)

"My friends, behold, I give unto you a revelation and commandment." (D&C 103:1.)

"My friends, fear not." (D&C 98:1.)

"I will call you friends, for you are my friends, and ye shall have an inheritance with me." (D&C 93:45.)

"And as I said unto mine apostles, even so I say unto you, for you are mine apostles, even God's high priests; ye are they whom my father hath given me; ye are my friends." (D&C 84:63.)

I bear you my witness our Lord and Savior Jesus Christ is our friend. In his loving processes of command, rebuke, greeting, revelation, encouragement, and long suffering, he daily proves this. Certainly he is willing to take us the way we are, but he wants to leave us improved in his word and his paths.

Enjoy with me some very simple yet powerful recent conversations I've had in seeking the true significance of friendship. I asked an eight-year-old girl, "Who is your best friend?" "My mommy," she replied. "Why?" "Because she is nice to me."

A priest-age young man was asked the same question. "My bishop." "Why?" "Because he listens to us."

143

A thirteen-year-old boy: "My Scoutmaster." "Why?" "He does everything with us."

A prisoner: "The chaplain." "Why?" "He believes me. He even believes me sometimes when he shouldn't have."

A husband: "My wife." "Why?" "Because she is the best part of me."

From these can we not conclude that friendship is earned?

It was Emerson who said, "The only way to have a friend is to be one." No one can be a friend until he is known. A friend is a person who will take the time not only to know us, but also to be with us. One of the finest presents each of us can give anyone is our best self. Joseph Smith gave us a glimpse of his measure of friends when he said, "If my life is of no value to my friends, it is of no value to me." The Savior said, "Greater love hath no man than this, that a man lay down his life for his friends." (John 15:13.) When Robert Louis Stevenson was asked the secret of his radiant, useful life, he responded simply, "I had a friend." In Exodus 33:11 we read, "The Lord spake unto Moses as a man speaketh unto his friend."

A friend in the true sense is not a person who passively nods approval. A friend is a person who cares.

No greater reward can come to any of us as we serve than a sincere "Thank you for being my friend." When those who need assistance find their way back through and with us, it is friendship in action. When the weak are made strong and the strong stronger through our lives, friendship is real. If a man can be judged by his friends, he can also be measured by their heights. How can we help a friend? An Arabian proverb helps us answer: "A friend is one to whom one may pour out all the contents of one's heart, chaff and grain together, knowing that the gentlest of hands will take and sift it, keep what is worth keeping, and with the breath of kindness blow the rest away."

Yes, a friend is a person who is willing to take me the way I am, but is willing and able to leave me better than he found me.

All of us should be eternally grateful for the classic experience shared by Peter and John when they approached the Gate Beautiful. A man, lame from birth, was lying there. A beggar all his life, he had never walked on his feet. As they moved in his direction he held out his hands beckoning, expecting alms. Peter said to him, "Silver and gold have I none; but such as I have give I thee: In the name of Jesus Christ of Nazareth rise up and walk. And he took him by the right hand, and lifted him up." (Acts 3:6.)

Peter was a friend. He told the beggar, "Rise and walk; I'm going to help you." We too must take the friend by the hand until he sees and finds that he has enough strength to go on his own. Is it not appropriate to conclude that Peter was willing to take the friend the way he was, but left him improved?

Our Savior pointed the way to reap friendship with our associates and with him when he declared: "For I was an hungred, and ye gave me meat: I was thirsty, and ye gave me drink: I was a stranger, and ye took me in. . . . Verily I say unto you, Inasmuch as ye have done it unto one of the least of these my brethren, ye have done it unto me." (Matthew 25:35, 40.)

I pray God to help us to be friends. We need God's friendship. He pleads for ours. God lives. He is near. He is available. Jesus Christ is our Redeemer and Savior, and he too is our friend.

The Power of Plainness

Recently in a study group of college-age students I was asked, "Which scripture or quotation in Church history gives you the greatest spiritual uplift?" Although I don't ever remember having been asked this question in such a setting before, I found myself answering without hesitation and with firm conviction: "I think the most powerful declaration ever uttered in the history of the Church is, *'This is My Beloved Son. Hear Him!'* " (Joseph Smith—History 1:17.)

We went on to talk about the powers of this celestial conversation and of the plainness of the setting, the greeting, the introduction, and the invitation. Here in a grove of trees two heavenly messengers were appearing to a fourteen-year-old boy in response to his earnest pleas and unwavering faith. Here in a setting of simple beauty an obscure boy was called by name by God, was introduced to the Savior Jesus Christ, and was invited to listen to words of understandable plainness that he might begin to learn the most important facts taught in this world.

The reality of this vision gives new significance to Nephi's declarations concerning plainness. "My soul delighteth in plainness unto my people, that they may learn." (2 Nephi 25:4.) "For my soul delighteth in plainness; for after this manner doth the Lord God work

147

among the children of men." (2 Nephi 31:3.) "I glory in plainness; I glory in truth; I glory in my Jesus, for he hath redeemed my soul from hell." Through this great prophet Nephi, along with other leaders and wise teachers, we come to realize that we learn more readily if principles are taught and explained in plainness. Brigham Young once said that if he could do but one thing to bless the Saints, he believed it would be to give them "eyes with which to see things as they are." (*Journal of Discourses* 3:221.)

Plainness is best comprehended by the humble, the teachable, the intelligent, the wise, and the obedient. Often plain truths are perverted by the pretentious, the crude, the low, the critical, the contentious, the haughty, and the unrighteous. More so than at any other time in our history, there is an urgency in today's society for men and women to step forward and teach the gospel of Jesus Christ in the power of plainness. God delights when his truths are taught clearly and understandably with no conspicuous ornamentation. Plainness in life, word, and conduct are eternal virtues. When the plainness of Christian teaching and living is lost, apostasy and suffering result. People walk in darkness when the light of plainness is taken from their lives.

"They have taken away from the gospel of the Lamb many parts which are plain and most precious; and also many covenants of the Lord have they taken away.

"And all this have they done that they might pervert the right ways of the Lord, that they might blind the eyes and harden the hearts of the children of men." (1 Nephi 13:26-27.)

The truths of the gospel of Jesus Christ are plain, precious, and powerful. The lives of the worthy are plain, precious, and powerful. May I share with you a few lessons taught in plainness for which I will eternally be grateful. Some of them come from young children who are humble and accepting in their pure faith. The

Savior taught that all mankind should become as little children if they would be the greatest in the kingdom of heaven. Now, an example of the power of plainness in prayer:

During one particularly difficult winter, the First Presidency asked the Latter-day Saints to observe a week of prayer so that "the ravages of hunger, illness, cold, and drought might be alleviated (now and in the days to come at home and abroad)." It was reported that, at the end of the week in a family home evening, an eight-year-old girl pleaded in her prayers for more snow so "there would be enough water next summer so the whole family could go swimming together." In the eyes of an eight-year-old, top priority was enough water for a family summer swim. Who is to say her prayer, given with plain, childlike faith, wasn't most acceptable as she asked for the possibility of family fun together?

The power of a plain, unadorned testimony is always impressive to me. I recall a twelve-year-old boy standing in front of a large congregation to share his testimony. He stood speechless; our hearts went out to him. The creeping seconds dragged on, making the silence of the moment intense. Prayerfully we hoped that he might gain composure and the ability to express his testimony. After great uneasiness and anxiety peculiar to a young person in such a circumstance, he raised his bowed head and softly said, "Brothers and sisters, my testimony is too small." He cleared his voice and sat down. His message had been given. I thought then, as I think now, what a timely observation. Whose testimony isn't too small? Whose testimony doesn't need to be added upon? After this one-sentence sermon, I acknowledged before the congregation that my testimony was too small also, and I was going to give it a chance to grow by more frequent sharing. I had been taught by a plain, simple statement.

Testimonies grow and lessons are taught in The Church of Jesus Christ of Latter-day Saints by plain and simple acts. On Sunday morning a young girl just barely out of Junior Sunday School, with her face shining, her hair carefully combed, dressed in her best, hesitatingly walks to the pulpit. Her little hand reaches up and pulls the microphone down to her level, and with a furtive look at her mother for courage, she leads the congregation in the sacrament gem. As time goes by, these plain acts become stepping-stones to poise, to testimony, and to a knowledge of the scriptures.

Each Sunday at the sacrament tables all over the world, priests dressed neatly, but not in robes or ornamentation, have the honor of blessing the sacrament. Deacons, with pride and reverence, in an orderly but simple way, pass the sacred emblems. These Aaronic Priesthood members are taught to watch and plan so no member is deprived of participation in this sacred ordinance. These same young men may be watching and caring for all ward members in all ways as, in the years to come, they serve as members of bishoprics.

Teenage young women involved in service projects as simple but as basic as visiting the sick or housebound or fellowshipping a nonmember friend will find these appropriate stepping-stones in reaching powerful and purposeful womanhood. Some of life's greatest lessons are taught and learned as we go about our Father's business in routine daily kindnesses.

Hundreds of teachers throughout the Church form car pools to transport distant children from school to Primary so they can be taught the plain and beautiful meaning of "I Am a Child of God." A new convert to the Church is asked to help with a Relief Society lesson or demonstration. Never before has she stood before a group of women. With support and encouragement from her understanding sisters she is able to fill one plain and simple assignment that could well lead her on her way to family and personal greatness and added opportunities for executive and teaching positions.

The power of plainness in discipline in the gospel of Jesus Christ is not always appreciated and understood, but to the repentant and remorseful, it is a great blessing. Discipline in the Church is plain, and repentance and forgiveness are available by following simple steps.

Not long ago a wise member was stopped in the hall of one of our ward buildings and asked in a hushed voice if she had heard that brother so-and-so had been excommunicated from the Church. When the sister indicated that she already knew of the situation, the talebearer said, "Isn't that awful!" To this her friend responded with, "No, I think it is wonderful. Now the burden can be lifted and he can start back with all of us helping and loving him." Here in simplicity and love was a lesson being taught by someone who could have been a contributor to idle, hurtful conversation.

In the life of Jesus Christ, each step along his path was plainly marked and plainly taught that we might learn. Recall with me if you will a few of his words spoken in powerful plainness as shared at random from the book of Matthew.

"Blessed are the meek." (Matthew 5:5.)

"Blessed are the merciful." (Matthew 5:7.)

"Love your enemies." (Matthew 5:44.)

"Thou shalt love thy neighbour as thyself." (Matthew 22:39.)

"He that findeth his life shall lose it; and he that loseth his life for my sake shall find it." (Matthew 10:39.)

"He that hath ears to hear, let him hear." (Matthew 11:15.)

"For what is a man profited, if he shall gain the whole world, and lose his own soul?" (Matthew 16:26.)

"Whosoever therefore shall humble himself as this little child, the same is the greatest in the kingdom of heaven." (Matthew 18:4.)

"Whosoever will be chief among you, let him be your servant." (Matthew 20:27.)

Certainly the Savior has spoken in plainness that we may learn. His words are eloquent in their plainness.

Glamour and mystery do not lead to eternal life. Some overlook the great rewards and the joys of the gospel because they feel that the gift of eternal life and the knowledge of the Savior can be attained only by ornamentation and mystery. The Lord has told us that we must learn line upon line and precept upon precept.

May we learn the plain and simple truths of the gospel by following the plain and simple steps outlined by our leaders. Each assignment filled and each lesson learned leads more surely to the celestial kingdom than do pomp, ceremony, and ostentation. Look not for glamour, but for humility in everyday service. Learn obedience and understanding from the plain truths of the gospel and then share them in candid, clear, and frank language and actions. The power of plainness in living and teaching is a delight to the mind and will of our Heavenly Father.

Rated A

One of life's more common experiences is to be rated or graded. Youngsters learn quickly whether or not their actions are acceptable to parents. Rewards or punishments can be quickly administered in the home, and such grading or rating by parents has a lot to do with the formation of ideals in living.

Those who enter school embark on a long struggle to achieve the kinds of grades that will make them acceptable to those among whom they must live and work. Those who become involved in military activities are soon caught up in a myriad of inspections and ratings.

When we accept employment we quickly realize that we are graded by the responsibilities given and the wages paid. Superior work is rewarded with higher pay and greater opportunities.

Those who manufacture goods or merchandise or produce food are rated by a variety of consumer organizations. "Grade A" products bring higher prices.

As part of a free government, we see the grading of leaders at each election.

In the media, subscriptions to newspapers and magazines provide an immediate public rating of their effectiveness. Television is particularly vulnerable to the ratings and gradings of professional organizations. Programs with poor ratings are usually doomed.

And so it goes on and on in almost everything we do in life. We have a tendency to rate or grade others, and they do the same to us. If our perspective is proper, we use these ratings or gradings to motivate us to reach high levels of achievement and self-discipline. The whole concept of ratings enables us to set high goals and provides the challenge to us to achieve them.

In spite of this inborn desire to achieve, there remains an area where the attainment of high or good ratings seems to be ignored. I speak of the growing numbers of movies, books, magazines, theatrical productions, and television programs in which efforts to glorify immorality or violence have become predominant. "Rated R" or "Rated X" has replaced the idealism of being "Rated A."

I know that free expression is a vital part of the eternal principle of free agency and must be preserved and protected. I also know how certain forces use the freedom of speech to degrade or debase, and this constitutes perversion and enslavement. Because I recognize that there will always be opposition in all things, I suspect that we will not soon see the day when obscenity in its various forms will be entirely eliminated. But I have faith that it can be fully eliminated in the lives of quality individuals. I firmly believe that most thinking people can be inspired to strive for the A rating by choosing wholesome, worthwhile literature, art, and habits.

As each of us uses our free agency to choose the material that enters our lives, we ought to recognize that the battle between "Rated A" and "Rated X" is part of the war that began in heaven and is still being fought today. The enemy seeks any strategic or tactical foothold he can gain, and any bridgehead he attains becomes the launching point for the next encounter. The number of victories we allow him can seriously affect the final outcome of the struggle.

How does the adversary wage this battle? What are his tactics? Those who are fighting pornography and obscenity have helped us recognize some of his battle plans. They tell us that a person who becomes involved in obscenity soon acquires distorted views of personal conduct. He becomes unable to relate to others in a normal, healthy way. Like most other habits, an addictive effect begins to take hold of him. A diet of violence or pornography dulls the senses, and future exposures need to be rougher and more extreme. Soon the person is desensitized and is unable to react in a sensitive, caring, responsible manner, especially to those in his own home and family. Good people can become infested with this material and it can have terrifying, destructive consequences.

One such young man who became a casualty of this conflict was a respected husband and community member. Someone with whom he worked brought lurid bits of pornography and passed them around the office. At first it was treated as a joke, and those who viewed them kidded each other about such things of the world. This young man, however, mainly out of curiosity, thought he should study them carefully in case he might have occasion to help others combat such evils of the world. As he looked at the items more and more frequently, he was overcome by a spirit of the adversary that he did not recognize. Soon he sought more pornographic materials from his fellow employe, and the two of them began to spend more time discussing these evil things.

Still thinking he was becoming enlightened as to the ways of the world so that he could be a stronger influence for good among his friends, this young man became trapped by his own ignorance of the enemy's ways. His associate convinced him that he should experiment with the actions portrayed in the materials he was viewing. With his spiritual sensitivity dulled, he agreed, and he approached his wife with the idea. She was surprised and shocked by his suggestions, and when he continued his insensitive pleas, she finally refused to have anything to do with him. In his distorted condition he sought gratification elsewhere, and in the end he lost her, his family, and his self-respect.

The scriptures help us understand the strategy and tactics of the enemy. Nephi in the Book of Mormon saw the conflict of our day and tells us plainly:

"For behold, at that day shall he rage in the hearts of the children of men, and stir them up in anger against that which is good.

"And others will he pacify, and lull them away into carnal security, that they will say: "All is well in Zion; yea, Zion prospereth, all is well—and thus the devil cheateth their souls, and leadeth them away carefully down to hell.

"And behold, others he flattereth away, and telleth them there is no hell; and he saith unto them: I am no devil, for there is none—and thus he whispereth in their ears, until he grasps them with his awful chains, from whence there is no deliverance." (2 Nephi 28:20-22.)

The great prophet Mormon, viewing his own fallen people, wrote his son Moroni a very telling indictment when he said that because of wickedness his people were "past feeling." (See Moroni 9:20.) How tragic to reach the point where the Spirit must withdraw, and we become unable to sense or feel right from wrong.

If we continue to lose skirmishes in the battle with Satan, the ultimate chains with which he grasps us will be as awful as the scriptures indicate. How awful this state is might be indicated by the words a dictionary uses to describe the word *obscenity*. Obscenity, it indicates, defiles, nauseates, offends, perverts, impairs, corrupts, infects, misleads, poisons, warps, weakens, and spoils. When I think of these words and then remember that the Prophet Joseph Smith admonished us to seek for things that are "virtuous, lovely, or of good report, or praiseworthy" (Article of Faith 13), I shudder at the blindness of so many.

In olden times the call to battle was the sure sound of a trumpet. The call to battle that I sound is a call to find so much that is wholesome or "Rated A" that there is no time or inclination for the carnal. It is a call to strive for a rating that can be remembered with joy forever.

First I challenge parents to be concerned about what your children read or view. Good reading begins at the bedside of your little ones. Never be too busy to read wholesome bedtime stories at the close of the day. Select from the classics of children's literature uplifting stories that can build noble ideals in your youngsters. I shall never forget the impact of a simple child's story about a little engine that thought he could, and then he did. How often I have said to myself, "I think I can, I think I can, I think I can," and then found growing within myself the personal power to do something good. Consider the difference in children who are cuddled and snuggled at bedtime by parents who read them stories from good books, and then kneel at their bedside in prayer, as compared to those who go to bed after having viewed a violent television program.

Next, I challenge grandparents to foster reading programs with your grandchildren. If you are close enough to be with them, read the books to them that will help develop character and ideals. If you're a distance away, send them books, old or new, with a personal invitation to read them and report how they like them.

Next I challenge youth to cooperate with parents who are concerned about your reading and your viewing. Be concerned yourself about what you take into your mind. Young people, you would never eat a meal of spoiled or contaminated food if you could help it, would you? Select your reading and your viewing carefully and in good taste.

157

Next, I challenge families to foster movie viewing that is wholesome. Parents should know the movies their children attend and children should attend only the movies they have parental permission to view. If movie viewing is an important part of your family life, and good ones are not available in commercial movie houses, wise parents will rent full-length movies that entertain and edify.

Next, I challenge every Latter-day Saint to come to a knowledge and an understanding of the scriptures. These sacred books are our bulwark of defense against a cunning adversary. Each person should own and use his personal copies of the scriptures. Take them to meetings and classes. Read them in leisure moments. Develop a careful plan of study and meditation. Take them on trips as well.

A friend of mine told me recently of his family vacation this past summer. A long distance was being driven, and the children, who ranged from preschoolers to high school age, grew restless. The parents had wisely taken along the scriptures, and when these restless times came, family members read chapters and then everyone talked about what had been read. The teenagers who did most of the reading quit teasing the little ones, and the little ones seemed very interested in what the older ones had to say. This family read a sizable part of the New Testament while traveling on their vacation.

The battle to be "Rated A" is a battle we can win. We do so many things in life that bring success that it seems incredible how easily we let the adversary weaken us by impure materials read or viewed.

My plea is that we will strive to be "Rated A" in all we do in life. We want good grades in school. We want to eat the best food we can get. I hope we will also strive to feed our minds with things that are lovely, wholesome, and praiseworthy.

The desire to achieve has been placed in us by a loving Creator who honors our free agency but nonetheless beckons to us to do well. He it is who will grade our eternal report card. The adversary would weaken and dull our senses so we lose sight of the final time of rating or judging. We are in a battle with evil powers who are cunning and crafty. They can lull us and pacify us through carnal things if we are not careful. But if we take the offense in the contest and seek those things which are praiseworthy, we can build an armor that will not be pierced.

So now, in the midst of this battle, let us sound our trumpets for that which is "Rated A": A for actions, A for achievement, and A for approbation, even that approbation from Him whose voice can say to us: "Well done, thou good and faithful servant: . . . enter thou into the joy of thy Lord." (Matthew 25:21.)

Be Patient in All Things

In section 6 of the Doctrine and Covenants, important instructions were given to Oliver Cowdery: "Therefore be diligent; stand by my servant Joseph, faithfully, in whatsoever difficult circumstances he may be for the word's sake. Admonish him in his faults, and also receive admonition of him. Be patient; be sober; be temperate; have patience, faith, hope and charity." (D&C 6:18-19.)

Please note the double emphasis on patience. Oliver, like all of us at times, apparently needed double reminding. He later fell because he lacked patience. He failed in the test of patience. He had handled the sacred plates; he had seen John the Baptist; he had received the higher priesthood from Peter, James, and John. He had participated in many unusual blessings, but he knew not patience.

Someone has said, "Patience is the support of weakness; impatience is the ruin of strength." Now let me share with you some thoughts about patience in four areas of our lives.

1. *Patience with God.* How often have we heard people say, "I cannot believe or put my trust in an unknown being who permits my mother, my father, my brother, my sister, my child to die or suffer when I know I am entitled to have my prayers answered, as are they. If there is a God, he surely would have answered my

161

prayers and heard my pleas." Aren't we lacking in
patience, to say the least, when we are inclined to tell
God how to answer our prayers and desires? Our relationship to God will improve as we learn to ask rather
than to tell. Surely it is wisdom that we seek not to
counsel the Lord. Aren't we out of our realm when we
judge or are inclined to second-guess God in our human
frailties?

"And again, be patient in tribulation." (D&C 54:10.)
Proper prayer teaches us patience. Often our prayers are
best answered in silence, and sometimes the answers to
our prayers are delayed so we may learn patience. Our
Heavenly Father is an almighty God because he has
eternal patience with us. God lives; he loves us; he hears
our prayers; he answers our prayers; he answers the
prayers of the faithful; he hears the prayers of the
repentant. God can be found if we have the patience to
seek, knock, ask, and listen.

2. *Patience with Family.* The apostle James said, "Let
every man be swift to hear, slow to speak, slow to
wrath." (James 1:19.) I think it was Seneca who said,
"The greatest remedy for anger is delay." Oh, that we
had the patience to withstand such family statements as
these:

"I am ashamed of you."

"I never want to see you again."

"You're a disgrace to the family."

"You've ruined our lives."

"What have we done to deserve such a son, or such a
daughter?"

"This is a fine way to treat us after all we have done
for you."

"You'll never amount to anything."

Yes, even "Get out and never come back."

I, along with you, wish that such statements were
never made. But if they are, do we have the patience to
withstand, forgive, and bear without malice?

A young woman I know decided upon marriage. When she consulted her father, he said, "Marriage will be a tremendous adjustment. Don't have any children until you have become adjusted to each other and know each other well." Her marriage was in difficulty after six months. As I visited with her, I thought to myself, speaking of patience with parents, "Maybe it would have been well if at the time, she had said to her father, who undoubtedly had given his advice in all sincerity, 'Father, if you don't mind, these are things my husband and I will work out, decide, and plan for ourselves.' " Patience with family members is most important.

Let me tell you about a young man I met at a religious service at the Utah State Prison. The inmates sat on one side of the hall and their relatives, families, and friends on the other side. As we entered through the rear door each individual was already seated, ready for the service to begin. I noticed a young man near the front nudge his buddy and ask, "Which one of those guys is Ashton?"

"Ashton's the one in the middle," his buddy said. We walked up toward the front, and as we reached the place where these young men were seated, this young questioning prisoner came over to me and said, "Could I talk to you for a moment?"

One of the deputy wardens walked over and told him to sit down, but he repeated his request, "I want to talk to Ashton."

I saw that he was determined, so when the deputy asked me, "Do you want to speak to him," I replied, "Yes, I do."

I'll never forget what the prisoner told me privately just before the service started. He took my arm and pointed over to the other side of the room.

"Do you see the guy on the end of the third row?" he asked. I looked over toward a man across the room. "He's my dad," I was told. "You know what?"

I asked, "What?"

He continued, "Next week my dad's going to be ordained an elder, and I'm the guy what's done it. Ever since I've been in this prison, my dad's been coming down once a week to see me. I've been teaching him out of the Book of Mormon and the Bible. Now he has shaped up and is ready to be ordained an elder."

I found out later that that young man had every right to say, "You see that man over on the end of the third row? He's my dad. I'd like to break his back. He's no good. He's the reason I am here. The only time he ever spent any time with me in my life was after I came here." But he didn't say those things. In the true spirit of patience, he accepted his father when he visited him, and now his father was qualified to be ordained an elder because his son had patiently worked with him.

After the meeting I asked him, "What are you going to do now that your father is going to be ordained an elder?"

With a serious look in his eyes he answered, "Now I'm going to start on my mom."

I was interviewing a missionary not long ago. In the privacy of a small room in the meetinghouse he asked me, "Brother Ashton, do you think I can make it as a missionary? I've been out here fourteen months. My father is an alcoholic. My mother's been divorced twice. Can I make it as a missionary?"

I asked, "How do you feel about your dad? How do you feel about your mother?"

His chin quivered as he replied, "I love them."

I felt impressed to say, "You'll make it. With patience and love like that you can't fail."

3. *Patience with Friends, Associates, and Neighbors.* Each of us needs to develop the patience not to resist reminders. We must be patient in counsel and in the repentance processes of our friends.

In John we find a passage of scripture that is seldom

used in the framework of patience, but it does fit this principle well:

"This is now the third time that Jesus shewed himself to his disciples, after that he was risen from the dead.

"So when they had dined, Jesus saith to Simon Peter, Simon, son of Jonas, lovest thou me more than these? He saith unto him, Yea, Lord; thou knowest that I love thee. He saith unto him, Feed my lambs.

"He saith to him again the second time, Simon, son of Jonas, lovest thou me? He saith unto him, Yea, Lord; thou knowest that I love thee. He saith unto him, Feed my sheep.

"He saith unto him the third time, Simon, son of Jonas, lovest thou me? . . ."

At this point the scriptures say that Peter was grieved, but I would like to suggest that perhaps Peter was impatient, "because he said unto him the third time, Lovest thou me? And he said unto him, Lord, thou knowest all things; thou knowest that I love thee. Jesus saith unto him, Feed my sheep." (John 21:14-17.) Oh, that we could take counsel and direction repeatedly without resentment and without impatience!

Let us never be in the position of giving people last chances: "Either—or else. I've put up with this as long as I can." Let us forgo giving last chances to family members or friends. This is not the spirit of Christ.

4. *Patience with Ourselves.* It is not our role to be self-condemning. I like to think that the admonition of the Savior, "judge not, that ye be not judged," has direct reference to us and our relationship with ourselves. We should not judge ourselves. We should teach ourselves patience—patience to believe in ourselves, patience to motivate ourselves, patience to believe that God and we can do it. When necessary, we should lean on the truth that we are children of God. God and we, with patience on our part, can do it. We do not have to worry about the patience of God, because he is the personification of

patience, no matter where we have been, what we have done, or what we have allowed ourselves to think of ourselves. Two of Satan's greatest tools are impatience and discouragement. Drugs, moral misconduct, and violent protest are merely evidences of internal impatience on our part.

"Blessed is the man that endureth temptation: for when he is tried, he shall receive the crown of life, which the Lord hath promised to them that love him.

"Let no man say when he is tempted, I am tempted of God: for God cannot be tempted with evil, neither tempteth he any man:

"But every man is tempted, when he is drawn away of his own lust, and enticed." (James 1:12-14.)

Patience is personal. Patience is a great teacher. Patience is a great achievement. Patience is a great power. I hope and pray that our Heavenly Father will help us to be patient with God, with our families, with our friends, associates, and neighbors, and, most of all, with ourselves. Our Heavenly Father is aware of each of us, and all he asks in return is for us to be patient with him.

Joseph Smith, in contrast to Oliver Cowdery, remained true and faithful and was a vital instrument in the hands of the Lord because his patience was unceasing and undying.

Man is that he might have joy, and we can have joy only as we practice patience. One of the primary reasons we have been placed here upon the earth is to know God through diligence and patience. May God help us to be patient in all things.

Who's Losing?

One warm summer evening Sister Ashton and I were enjoying a baseball game. During the early part of the competition, our attention was diverted from the action by a late arriver. As he walked by, he spotted me and asked, "Who's losing?" I responded with, "Neither one." Following my answer, he glanced at the right-field scoreboard, noticed the game wasn't tied, and walked on, undoubtedly wondering about me. Seconds after he made his way to his seat, Sister Ashton said, "He doesn't know you very well, does he?" "What makes you say that?" She replied, "If he did, he would know you don't believe anyone is losing. Some are ahead and some are behind, but no one is losing. Isn't that right?" I smiled in approval with a warm feeling inside.

All of us, young and old, will do well to realize that attitude is more important than the score. Desire is more important than the score. Momentum is more important than the score. The direction in which we are moving is more important than position or place.

The truth "For as he thinketh in his heart, so is he" (Proverbs 23:7) is as applicable today as any time in history. I remember years ago meeting a young man who had tattooed on his body the words "BORN LOSER." I don't think you'll be surprised to learn I met him in a state prison. I also remember once asking two young boys if they could swim. One said, "No." The other, "I don't know. I've never tried." Unknowingly, perhaps their attitudes were showing.

Proper attitude in this crisis-dominated world is a priceless possession. Never before has it been more important for all of us to move forward with conviction. We may be behind, but we are not losing if we are moving in the right direction. God will not score our performances until the end of the journey. He, who made us, expects us to be victorious. He stands by anxious to answer our call for help. Sad, but true, many today are behind in their contacts with God, and are encouraging destructive attitudes toward self and fellowmen. We need to lead with good cheer, optimism, and courage if we are to move onward and upward.

The truths, ". . . in everything give thanks" (D&C 98:1), "Thou shalt thank the Lord thy God in all things" (D&C 59:7), and "he who receiveth all things with thankfulness shall be made glorious" (D&C 78:19), are not only recommended tools of appreciation, but are also powerful attitude guidelines prescribing rewarding patterns. Think of the personal challenge to thank God in all things. If we thank God in all things, we will not permit ourselves to get behind. We must work each day to beat yesterday's record—not someone else's. With his help we can accomplish all things and be winners indeed in the processes of eternity.

We must strive for an ingrained attitude of self-confidence that will make us believers in self. How important it is in all our lives to develop an appropriate balance of self-confidence and humility. Proper self-confidence lets every man know there is a spark of divinity within wanting to be nurtured in meaningful growth. Proper attitude enables us to live in harmony with our potentials.

We must beware of pride. An egotist will never get anywhere in this world because he thinks he's already there. Someone has said, "Egotism is the anesthetic that dulls the pain of stupidity." Egotism can be cancerous to the soul. The attitude with which we approach each day certainly controls the outcome. We must be more concerned over what we do with what happens to us than with what happens to us. Proper attitude toward self is an eternal pursuit. Positive personal attitude will insist we deliver our best, even though less might seem adequate for the moment. Proper attitude toward self demands we be realistic—tough with ourselves and self-disciplining.

Let me share with you a verse from a nineteenth century writer, Josiah Gilbert Holland. The bust of Dr. Holland is in the Hall of Fame in New York, and beneath is this powerful verse he wrote, entitled "Wanted":

God give us men! A time like this demands
Strong minds, great hearts, true faith, and ready hands;
Men whom the lust of office does not kill;
Men whom the spoils of office cannot buy;
Men who possess opinions and a will;
Men who love honor; men who will not lie.

Proper attitude is a prerequisite to quality performance. We need men with the courage to put proper attitudes into action. We need more men today with patience and purposeful endurance. We need more men with the fearless conviction of Joseph Smith.

When the Lord instructed us to be anxiously engaged in a good cause, the importance of enthusiasm was being reemphasized. Great things are accomplished by those moving forward in enthusiasm. To the scripture, "let us cheerfully do all things that lie in our power," for our purposes we would add the words "and enthusiastically" to have it appropriately move us: "Therefore, . . . let us cheerfully *and enthusiastically* do all things that lie in our power." Cheerfully Jesus "went about doing good, and healing all that were oppressed by the devil; for God was with him." (Acts 10:38.) Only through proper attitude will we, too, be able to love our enemies and bless them that curse us. (See Matthew 5:44.)

Another important ingredient of proper attitude is resilience—the ability to cope with change. Adaptability cushions the impact of change or disappointment. Love can be a great shock absorber as we adjust in trials and tragedy.

We need to constantly build hope in ourselves and those about us. We need to personally make dark days brighter. Isn't it a joy, a lift, a light to see someone with heavy challenges and burdens moving forward to victory in the only contest that really matters. Hope makes it possible for us to know that even in temporary failure or set-back there is always a next time, even a tomorrow. One of the greatest tragedies of our time is children of God—you and I—living and performing below our capabilities.

Strength and courage come when we realize the words "Come, follow me," were spoken by a living Savior of hope and trust who extended the invitation to us without regard to where we are or have been. His was the perfect example. His was the perfect attitude. His was the perfect life. He would be true to his calling at whatever the cost. His labors, his life, and his teachings are cherished possessions. Our pathways are clearly marked, thanks to his steps. His experiences are our strengths. I have many times told our missionaries that it is not so important whether a young man has been through the experiences of a mission as it is whether the mission experience has been through him.

Though he, Jesus, was a son busily engaged in his Father's business, he was never too busy to assist a troubled mother, a sick man, a friend, a little child. These attitudes, these services were but outward evidence of inward greatness. As we too learn to serve, as did he, we learn to live abundantly. A proper attitude helps us find God through service to his children.

Nazareth was little and looked down upon. It bore the brunt of ridicule. It had not been the scene of historic achievement. It had produced no winners. "Can there any good thing come out of Nazareth?" (John 1:46.) His attitude, his works, his life lifted the little village out of obscurity. "Jesus of Nazareth," the world later called him, bringing honor to a once-despised town. Once rejected by his own, the will, the way, and the work would yet identify him as King of kings and Lord of lords. He experienced scorn, ridicule, and abuse, but victory and triumph were his because he was busily engaged in good works. To those who would destroy, defeat, and discourage, he taught that truth shall triumph. To those who would desecrate his temples, he fearlessly declared, "Is it not written, My house shall be called of all nations the house of prayer? but ye have made it a den of thieves." (Mark 11:17.) His words and actions in this circumstance were but yet another evidence of character, conviction, courage, and proper attitude.

Every person in the world who loves courageous performance and appreciates proper attitude should read and reread the final chapters of the Savior's life. He lived, this Prince of Peace, in true majesty. When his relatives turned from him, his home town scorned his achievements, his best friend had died doubting, his disciples had turned away, and his enemies were about to triumph—so they supposed—what was his attitude? Was it one of complaining, faultfinding, retaliation, or defeat? Never! His majestic words were, "Let not your heart be troubled. . . . I have overcome the world." (John 14:1; 16:33.)

In the final week of his life, cries turned from "Hosanna" to "Crucify." Unwavering courage carried him onward and upward triumphantly. The honest in heart would yet know what he stood for and why he must die. Final scenes from the last week of his earthly life unfold for us lessons in greatness in attitude. Learn with me more of his courage and divinity as we see him continue faithfully to the end in those trying days. Recall with me the Last Supper with his disciples, a visit to the Garden for high communion with his Father—"Let this cup pass, nevertheless thy will be done" (Matthew 26:39)—a victory signal following the battle, and the crucifixion sight with soldiers appearing on the scene. When they boldly confronted him, prepared for resistance and rebellion, he greeted them with the question, "Whom seek ye?" Then he answered proudly, "I am he." (John 18:4-5.)

On a barren hill not far beyond the city wall he was nailed to a cross. As he suffered his cruel crucifixion, no doubt there were witnesses and spectators who observed with their limited perspective, "He is losing. He is confined. He is defeated." How wrong they were and are! Jesus of Nazareth a loser? Never! He is our Savior, our Redeemer, a winner, a Son of God.

This day he would have us permanently adopt the attitude of conviction and commitment so movingly expressed in verse seven of one of our hymns, "How Firm a Foundation":

> The soul that on Jesus hath leaned for repose
> I will not, I cannot, desert to his foes;
> That soul, though all hell should endeavor to shake,
> I'll never, no never, no never forsake!

—*Hymns,* no. 66

What a pleasure it is for me to bear special witness to his reality, strength, divinity, and earthly purposes. This is his church. This is his gospel. This is his plan for those who would conquer self, continue faithfully, and be victorious.

"He Isn't Worth His Feed"

For excitement, challenge, and diversion, a friend of mine hunted mountain lions in the hilltop areas of southern Utah. Among other things, this sport requires personal patience, endurance, and skill, durable horses, and dependable, well-trained dogs. To be effective in locating and cornering or "treeing" a mountain lion, dogs must be completely dependable from the moment the hunt starts until the capture is finished.

A few years ago when I was visiting with my friend at his place of business, I noticed he had a beautiful hunting dog tied to the outside of his office building. As I came close to the dog, I was impressed with his stature, markings, and color. I commented to the owner, "Isn't he a beauty? How long have you had him?"

"I've raised him from a pup. He's been trained since he was a few months old to track mountain lions," said the owner. "But now he's got to go. I'm going to get rid of him. He isn't worth his keep anymore."

"Why do you want to sell a dog as alert and strong as this one?" I asked.

To this query, the wise owner, a veteran of many mountain lion hunts, said with emphasis, "You know, when I have spent months and months training a hunting dog for these outings, I expect and demand one thing. When we're tracking lions, we're tracking lions, and that's it. My dogs—and I usually take about four of them—know this, and if one lets me down, he's had it. Last time we were out on a hunt, moving into the mountain areas where the lions hide out, this dog was distracted by a jack rabbit and ran after him for more than half an hour. Later on the same day he was gone for about an hour chasing a deer. Both of these incidents were indulged in by this disobedient dog despite many months of tedious training. I therefore resolved that when I returned to the city he would no longer be a member of the hunting expedition. He isn't worth his feed. He must be sold."

As I traveled back to Salt Lake City alone by automobile later that day, my thoughts turned to this experience with a master's comment and decision about one of his dogs. The dog had lost his usefulness because he had forgotten his training and the purpose of the hunt. He could be distracted, diverted, and led in wrong pursuits.

I recalled that similarly in our daily lives we sometimes forget our goals and purposes and let distractions, interferences, and temptations lead us away from the charted courses we have been trained to pursue. It is to be hoped that we will stay close to our Master, heeding his teachings and avoiding situations that tend to lead us away.

Lofty standards of behavior will always be based upon a love for the right and walking in paths of righteousness. Wickedness in any form will never lead to happiness. We must be aware of those who will deceive and have us believe there is no heaven, there is no hell, and that the only road to happiness is marked with compromise, convenience, and momentary pleasures or pursuits. Satan is real and he is effective. He would throw men down by his cunning. He would have all mankind strangers to God. Let us not be deceived. God lives, and through him and with him we can accomplish all things. We must not permit ourselves to become entangled in sin or to compromise our standards, but rather we must learn to avoid all the ways of Satan. His paths lead to disappointment, frustration, and regret.

We compromise our blessings and rationalize ourselves out of the sure and eternal ways when we do not ask our God to help us continue in his paths. Often a disciple of God can best be identified by the paths he travels. "If ye continue in my word, then are ye my disciples indeed; and ye shall know the truth, and the truth shall make you free." (John 8:31-32.)

The Lord has promised us he will help in our pursuit of happiness if we will continue the quest of righteousness and follow his paths. The abundant life will be ours if we walk with his strength. If we will remember and practice the Savior's teachings every day, Satan can have no power over us. God's strength makes it possible for us to walk uprightly.

Our continuing pursuit for happiness will bring us our Heavenly Father's strength and protection. In his paths we will find security. Let us not forget our goals and purposes, and let us not allow distractions, interferences, or temptations to lead us away from the charted courses we have been trained to pursue.

Our Eternal Family Home Storage Plan

It is true that "man doth not live by bread only, but by every word that proceedeth out of the mouth of the Lord doth man live." (Deuteronomy 3:3.) Home storage is sometimes best performed by casting our bread upon the waters rather than in the freezer. The only real home storage items we can take with us are ourselves and our families. Once stored, these things can constantly be shared and our supply will never be depleted. We need to be anxiously involved in the type of family storage that will sustain eternal life, "laying up in store for ourselves a good foundation against the time to come, that we may lay hold on eternal life." (1 Timothy 6:19.)

Luke tells us that "life is more than meat, and the body is more than raiment." (Luke 12:23.) Happiness is more important than money. Certain gifts and powers we possess are far more important than money. Money cannot buy those priceless gifts we have in our possession to store and share. In the past a great deal has been said about money and the importance of proper money management, but money makes available none of the basics of the kind of family storage I believe to be of the greatest importance. Let me illustrate with a personal experience.

Some months ago we had the opportunity of being in Suva, Fiji. I was surprised after registering at a motel to have the clerk say, "Elder Ashton, could my husband and I and our children visit with you tonight?" I didn't know that she knew who I was. I told her that we had meetings until ten o'clock in the evening, and she said, "We'll come then." That evening the woman, whose name is Jessie, and her husband and six children crowded into our motel room. After proper introductions, she led off with this question: "Our son is nineteen years of age. The question we want to ask you, Elder Ashton, is, should we continue to save our money so our son can go into the mission field, or should we continue to save our money so some day all of us can go to the temple in New Zealand and be sealed to each other?" My answer was, "In the Church we do both." Another question: "Is it true that some missionaries can get help from other families for assistance when the missionary's own family doesn't have very much money?" I said, "Yes, that is possible, but never deprive your family of the opportunity of taking part in some way to furnish money regularly to your missionary son. Do not let that opportunity escape your family no matter how slight the contribution."

Money, like people, is valuable only when it is put to worthy purposes. In this case, money will be nothing more than a means to an end. It is not money, but a lack of it, that is making this family strong. Within a few weeks Sister Ashton and I had a letter from Suva, Fiji, indicating that the nineteen-year-old son was serving in the mission field.

Just after we returned from Fiji, I had a private talk with my six-year-old grandson. I said, "Michael, I know a good man who lives on an island a long way from here, out in the Pacific Ocean. He's old enough to go on a mission, but he doesn't have enough money. Would you like to help him?" "Yeah, I'll help him. My mom and dad will too." "Michael, how much would you like to give?" "Would a quarter be all right?" Now you and I know that Michael's quarter is not much, but his willingness to give and share is what counts. We need to teach our youngsters in the home today that it is not enough to save for a mission: they should also have the opportunity to assist others who may not be able to save or to have the advantage of home life that recommends saving for a mission.

May I share another recent experience to illustrate the values as well as the opportunities of proper home storage by using the occasions of the day to store as we share and grow.

During a stake conference assignment, I was accompanied by a Regional Representative of the Twelve. As we flew between Salt Lake City and San Francisco, I was interested in his telling me about his wife, three sons, and two daughters. One daughter, the youngest of the five children, had passed away within the past year. At birth she suffered severe brain damage, and as a result, in the sixteen years of her life, she was never able to grow or develop. Constant care from a loving mother, patience and warmth from a kind father, and understanding from three noble brothers and a thoughtful sister made her presence special in the family. I was moved to new depths of understanding when this traveling companion told me what a blessing this soul had been to their household. He said, "Nothing that money could buy could have ever brought us together in love, patience, and humility as taking care of her did." Here was a tragedy, a trial, turned into an opportunity for blessings for eternal family storage and sharing. I thank this noble father, mother, and children for sharing with me out of their home storage.

Let me share with you another choice experience. It has to do with a calling of a new patriarch. I asked this good brother following the call, "If you had your choice, where would you like to have your ordination take place?" "Elder Ashton," he said, "we will come to your

179

office." "That isn't what I asked you," I said. "Where of all the places would you choose to have your ordination take place?" He replied, "As long as you put it that way, we would love to have it take place in our home with our children and grandchildren present."

Sister Ashton and I went to their home and participated in an enlarged family home evening. We heard children pay appropriate tribute to a deserving father and heard grandchildren say, "Grandpa is neat." At the close of the hour, all expressed deep appreciation for this choice experience. It was a long-to-be remembered evening for us. As Sister Ashton and I drove back home, our thoughts were turned to the fact that proper home experiences with children, mother, father, and even grandmother and grandfather are priceless. We have another evidence of the wisdom in the Doctrine and Covenants: "and visit the house of each member, and exhort them to pray vocally and in secret and attend to all family duties." (D&C 20:47.) Here again is home storage of eternal significance going forward.

May I share another experience. In Tonga during a missionary preparation session, with a twinkle in my eye, I was impressed to say jokingly to the fulltime missionaries, "Perhaps one of the best ways to increase our baptisms and convert all of the people of Tonga would be for one of you lady missionaries at a later date to become acquainted with the king's son, fall in love with him, and start the process of conversion from the top level."

To this quip, one of the native Tongan lady missionaries in broken English stood up and said, "None of us would go with him, Elder Ashton. He doesn't hold a temple recommend." My mind went again to money, children, mother, father, husband, and wife. Here was a beautiful young lady missionary teaching the lesson that a happy home with children, mother, and father is much more important than earthly possessions.

These attitudes, properly stored and shared, whether they be by missionaries or students or leaders, will prevent spiritual famine.

Let me share part of a letter recently received to again indicate how it is possible on a continuing basis to store as we share eternal goods.

"Dear Elder Ashton: At the beginning of the conference session, as I sat meditating, I was overwhelmed with the beauty of the people in attendance and the spirit I felt, but I was still tremendously sad. I knew the talks would all be about the importance of children, and I felt I was a failure as a mother. When you spoke, even though there were thousands in the building, I knew you were talking just to me. You said we are never failures until we give up on family members and weary in well doing. You also said that our trials and experiences with our own children will make us more sensitive to the problems of other children whom we may later be called upon to serve and lead. I pray that our Heavenly Father will bless our son. It was not his fault that his father and I made mistakes in rearing him. And since he has helped us to better understand other boys, he has done us a good service the hard way. Our son is sixteen. Every time I feel sad, I will remember what you said. We will try to lift others wherever God chooses us to serve without apology and without regret. Thank you for what you have done for me."

I have never met the lady who wrote this letter, but wherever she is, I take this opportunity to publicly thank her for her attitude, her priceless lesson on life— children, mother, father, and true values. Certainly money could not buy the wisdom she shares and stores.

In regard to this family situation, may I share a statement I made in general conference a few years ago: "I believe we start to fail in the home when we give up on each other. We have not failed until we have quit trying. As long as we are working diligently with love, patience, and long-suffering, despite the odds or the apparent lack of progress, we are not classified as failures in the home. We only start to fail when we give up on a son, daughter, mother, or father"—and may I add a husband or a wife. I believe this with all of my heart. This kind of home storage that is possible for us to accumulate will never be nil so long as we don't give up.

In the days ahead may we not only think of the basics of family food storage, but more importantly, the eternal basics not available through money. The only real home storage we can take with us is ourselves and our families. This kind of home storage is replenished as it is shared, and we are able to share only that which we have.

May the Lord help us to be prudent in our daily storage and in our sharing processes and to realize that only through children, mother, father, husband, and wife relationships can eternal home storage be realized. This type of family home storage doesn't cost money, but the benefits will go on through eternity.

A Time of Urgency

Picture with me in your mind's eye, if you will, a church building with a sign reading "Spiritual Fuel Available. No rationing, no stamps, no quotas. Come and prepare." Picture with me further a home with a welcome mat bearing the inscription "Welcome, Neighbor. Spiritual oil available. Come in as you are." Picture with me still further an individual whose very countenance radiates the words "I know God lives. My cup runneth over."

We are living in a time of urgency. We are living in a time of crisis. We are living in a time close to midnight. There is an urgency to meet the worldwide spiritual crisis through action now. It can only be accomplished by performance. Procrastination is a deadly weapon of human progress. Thank God there is no need of a shortage in the oil of preparedness. It is accumulated at will, drop by drop, in righteous living.

Jesus, our Redeemer, has given to us for our use in this day a powerful parable to stress the importance of constant personal preparedness. It is known as the Parable of the Ten Virgins, a warning to all mankind everywhere.

"Then shall the kingdom of heaven be likened unto ten virgins, which took their lamps, and went forth to meet the bridegroom.

"And five of them were wise, and five were foolish.

"They that were foolish took their lamps, and took no oil with them:

"But the wise took oil in their vessels with their lamps.

"While the bridegroom tarried, they all slumbered and slept. And at midnight there was a cry made, Behold, the bridegroom cometh; go ye out to meet him.

"Then all those virgins arose, and trimmed their lamps.

"And the foolish said unto the wise, Give us of your oil; for our lamps are gone out.

"But the wise answered, saying, Not so; lest there be not enough for us and you: but go ye rather to them that sell, and buy for yourselves.

"And while they went to buy, the bridegroom came; and they that were ready went in with him to the marriage: and the door was shut. Afterward came also the other virgins, saying, Lord, Lord, open to us.

"But he answered and said, Verily I say unto you, I know you not.

"Watch therefore, for ye know neither the day nor the hour wherein the Son of man cometh." (Matthew 25:1-13.)

It can be appropriately concluded the ten virgins represent the people of the Church of Jesus Christ, and not alone the rank and file of the world. The wise and foolish virgins, all of them, had been invited to the wedding supper; they had knowledge of the importance of the occasion. They were not pagans, heathens, or gentiles, nor were they corrupt or lost; rather they were informed people who had the saving, exalting gospel in their possession, but had not made it the center of their lives. They knew the way but were foolishly unprepared for the coming of the bridegroom. All had been warned their entire lives. All, even the foolish ones, trimmed their lamps at his coming, but their oil was used up; and in the moment when they needed it most, none was available to refill their lamps.

Thousands of us today are in a similar position. Through lack of patience and confidence, preparation has ceased. Others have lulled themselves into complacency with the rationalization that midnight will never come. The responsibility for having oil in our personal lamps is an individual requirement and opportunity. The oil of spiritual preparedness cannot be shared. The wise were not unkind or selfish when they refused oil to the foolish in the moment of truth. The oil could have been purchased at the market in the parable, but in our lives it is accumulated by righteous living, a drop at a time.

How can one share the blessing that comes through visiting the sick? How can one share the blessings that come from assisting the widowed or fatherless? How can one share a personal testimony? How can one share the blessing of attendance at a general conference? How can one share the lesson of obedience learned in living the principle of tithing? Certainly each must accumulate this kind of oil for himself. Let us not procrastinate. Midnight is so far and yet so close to those who have procrastinated. "But behold, your days of probation are past; ye have procrastinated the day of your salvation until it is everlastingly too late, and your destruction is made sure." (Helaman 13:38.)

There is an urgency in this day for us to prepare for the coming of the Lord. Great blessings are in store for those who have heeded the warning and continue in their preparations to accumulate the oil of righteousness in their lamps. In modern-day revelation the Lord has told us:

"And at that day, when I shall come in my glory, shall the parable be fulfilled which I spake concerning the ten virgins.

"For they that are wise and have received the truth,

and have taken the Holy Spirit for their guide, and have not been deceived—verily I say unto you, they shall not be hewn down and cast into the fire, but shall abide the day.

"And the earth shall be given unto them for an inheritance; and they shall multiply and wax strong, and their children shall grow up without sin unto salvation." (D&C 45:56-58.)

Now go back again with me in your thoughts to that church building I mentioned earlier with its sign of "Spiritual Fuel Available. . . . Come and prepare." Each of us undoubtedly has a different building in mind. Perhaps yours is the one you attend most frequently— your own ward or branch. One that I have in mind is the Masterton Ward in the Wellington New Zealand Stake.

I had the opportunity of dedicating this choice house of worship a few years ago. Never had I been in a building so immaculately clean. It looked new. It smelled new. It was beautiful in its simplicity. It was worthy in appearance to be dedicated to the Lord. It was built by our people, paid for by our people. It was polished to a fine finish by hands that took pride. It was tastefully landscaped and structually sound. According to the town mayor, a nonmember, it was built by a happy people.

Three weeks before our arrival it was predicted by some it couldn't possibly be ready. Those so inclined to doubt didn't know the good bishop and his ward family—people of humble circumstances but powerfully committed. Walls were painted and floors waxed by parents after their children had been put to sleep for the night. Young boys carried buckets of water to make the lawns green and the flowers bloom around the chapel because New Zealand had been long without rain. It was not only completed, it was shining! As these ward members worked together to meet the midnight hour, their love for each other was nurtured. They too shone in their triumph. Here was a group of people accumulating oil for their lamps a drop at a time through sacrifice, preparation, cooperation, faith, and works.

In all of our ward and stake buildings spiritual oil is available. Come and prepare. Join the ward members. Be involved. Don't simply give—give of yourself. Don't take without taking part. One who is thinking of others and serving others is filling his lamp with oil.

While our worldwide fuel energy crisis is relieved by conservation, the spiritual crisis, quite to the contrary, is corrected through use and preparation. The more you give, the more drops of spiritual oil you accumulate for yourself.

I am thinking now of a certain home, the home of a neighbor—your friend and mine. He certainly is one whose home is appropriately identified as one carrying the greeting "Welcome, neighbor. Spiritual oil available. Come in as you are." I refer to the home of our beloved President Spencer W. Kimball. Wherever we are, wherever we have been, he is our friend. His is a home of prayer. When he prays we feel the Lord's power near. Faith precedes his prayers. Those of us who have the great blessing of daily, intimate association with President Kimball have heard him observe that with each passing day prayer in his life has a new dimension. Prayer is a learning experience. Prayer is a power experience. Prayer is a humbling experience. Prayer is a resource for spiritual fuel. May we not appropriately conclude that though he, Spencer W. Kimball, is a prophet of God, yet learned he to pray by praying. He has wisely told us, "Attendance at sacrament meetings adds oil to our lamps, drop by drop, over the years. Fasting, family prayer, home teaching, control of bodily appetites, preaching the gospel, studying the scriptures— each act of dedication and obedience is a drop added to our store. Deeds of kindness, payment of offerings and tithes, chaste thoughts and actions, marriage in the

187

covenant for eternity—these too contribute importantly to the oil with which we can at midnight refuel our exhausted lamps."

I bear witness to you that God listens to humble prayers. If he didn't he wouldn't ask us to pray. Part of our worthwhile urgency, prayers today can be a reverent, quiet, listening period. Can we not appropriately say that he who goes to the well of prayer with faith unwavering is daily drawing oil for his lamp? It is also possible to help accumulate our supply in meaningful meditation.

Once more, think with me of those individual acquaintances who radiate active dedication in God's kingdom. It is a thrill to associate with them. It is a lift to feel of their enthusiasm and preparation in being about His business. I am thinking of a beautiful twenty-two-year-old woman, a convert of two years, whom Sister Ashton and I met in California. She is so excited about her recently discovered, priceless possession—the gospel of Jesus Christ—it is thrilling to be around her. There is a sincere urgency on her part to share the gospel with her associates, particularly her wonderful parents and family. As she prepares and performs, she accumulates oil for her lamp. There is no doubt in our minds she knows that God lives and Jesus is the Christ. Her cup is truly running over with that blessed knowledge and conviction.

When she so sweetly and yet so earnestly asked us if we couldn't find a few minutes to come and visit with her parents in their lovely home, we felt an urgency to be available at once. There was good fellowship in the home. Peace, unity, and love were there within its walls. "How wonderful my twenty-two years have been," she later wrote, "so challenging and rewarding. My blessings have been countless, and I am very thankful to my Heavenly Father. He blessed me with parents I love dearly and opportunities very few receive. The Church and gospel inspire me to work very hard in everything I do—especially in living a good life and sharing my many blessings with others."

Here is one of God's choicest daughters aware of the importance of now, right now, and the truths as recorded in Alma 34:32: "For behold, this life is the time for men to prepare to meet God; yea, behold the day of this life is the day for men to perform their labors."

We are living in a time of urgency. We are living in a time of spiritual crisis. We are living in a time close to midnight. "Wherefore, stand ye in holy places, and be not moved, until the day of the Lord come; for behold, it cometh quickly, saith the Lord." (D&C 87:8.)

I pray our Heavenly Father to daily assist us in our preparations that we may accumulate the oil of spirituality drop by drop in our constant pursuit in righteous living. The signs are available to us if we will but look. Thanks to the mercy and kindness of God we can say, "Spiritual Fuel Available. No rationing, no stamps, no quotas. Come and prepare." Through proper preparing and performing from within the walls of our homes, we can appropriately add, "Welcome, neighbor. Spiritual oil available. Come in as you are."

Index

Acting compared with reacting, 47

Actions: letting others dictate our, 47-48; love must be demonstrated through, 51-52, 53

Activating friends in the Church, 42-43, 101

Adam, 29

Adaptability, 170

Adulterous woman taken before Christ, 94-95

Airplane, woman smoking on, 82-83

Alms, beggar asked, of Peter and John, 121, 145

Ammon, 20, 27, 134-35

Apology, sincere, from parent to child, 63-64

Apostasy: due to murmuring, 85; when plainness is lost, 148

Appreciation: indicates maturity, 99; failure to show, offends God, 99; importance of, in marriage, 102; showing, by our lives, 102; shapes attitudes, 168

Artist who painted without hands, 90

Astronauts, 49

Athlete, great, performs for himself as well as for others, 105

Attitude: importance of, 168; as a prerequisite to good performance, 169

Baseball game, 167

Basketball game, 88-89

Battle against sin, 157

Blessings: should be counted every day, 11; come by obedience to law, 29

Brewing alcoholic beverages, man with degree in, 96

Brown, Hugh B., 41-42, 129

Brown, Zina Card, 41-42

Budget, 116

Building contractor, 54

Cancer, 43-44

Cannon, Christine Jacobsen, 43

Chastity, 19

Childlike faith, 33-34

Children: rearing of, 25; deaf, sing at stake conference, 89-90; should be involved in family financial concerns, 114; teaching value of work to, 114-15; reading with, 157

Christ. *See* Jesus Christ

Church of Jesus Christ of Latter-day Saints: helping others be committed to, 42-43; must state its positions without being contentious, 68

Churchill, Winston, 141-42

Clothing, importance of, to self-image, 106-7

Comforter, Christ promises to send, 21

Commandments, emphasis on, by adding "now," 13

Communication: through family home evening, 32; builds understanding, 32-33;